MW01199011

Friends Beyond Borders

Cultural Variations in Close Friendship

Roger Baumgarte

Friends Beyond Borders

Dedication

I would like to dedicate this book to the thousands of university students and people of all ages who have completed my friendship surveys. Most of these surveys were quite long, requiring 30 minutes or longer to complete, an investment of time most of you offered with enthusiasm. I'm humbly grateful for the faith you've shown in the value of this enterprise.

Contents

Preface

Until now, most publications related to research into cross-cultural friendships have been academic in nature. Roger Baumgarte's *Friends Beyond Borders* breaks this mold by offering a perspective that is solidly grounded in research, yet easy to read and highly entertaining.

When I first arrived in the United States as a German graduate student, I was enthused to learn all I could about U.S. culture by making friends with Americans. I had American roommates, joined the university choir and soon felt part of the community. Later I learned that not all international students have such positive experiences; in fact, more than a third have no American friends at all. Intrigued, I chose intercultural friendship as the subject of my doctoral dissertation, which resulted in the book *Intercultural Friendship: A Qualitative Study*. In the years since, I have continued research in the field and discovered— through my work and that of others—what far-reaching benefits intercultural friendships can have.

But making friends across cultures is a complex process influenced by many factors. *Friends Beyond Borders* explores these factors in a way that will be a worthwhile read for general audiences as well as students and researchers. The book draws on findings from psychology and intercultural communication to examine friendship and cultural variations.

Friends Beyond Borders is unique because it introduces friendship styles that differentiate the United States from contrasting cultures. In doing so, Roger Baumgarte tackles one of the most confounding questions in intercultural research. In accounts of U.S. culture, ranging from de Tocqueville's to current guidebooks for study-abroad students, Americans and their friendship patterns are often described as open and friendly, but lacking in depth and commitment. Baumgarte identifies original friendship styles that serve to explain this phenomenon.

The three styles typical in the U.S. (*Independent*, *Includer*, and *Idealist*) are contrasted with styles common in other cultures (*Intervener*, *Excluder*, and *Realist*). He points out that traits desired in close friends depend on one's cultural background. Friendship behaviors perceived as fun in *Independent* friendships, for example, can be perceived as shallow in *Intervener* cultures. Likewise, what is seen as caring by *Interveners* may be seen as overbearing by *Independents*.

By thoroughly analyzing each contrasting style, Baumgarte sheds light on cultural characteristics as well as core processes of effective intercultural communication. He brings the topic to life with personal anecdotes from sojourns in France and South Korea, astute observations, and case studies that illustrate particular complex points. Occasional pithy, funny, and thought-provoking quotes on friendship, language, and life provide a counterpoint, give pause, and enrich the narrative.

In addition to exploring friendship styles, *Friends Beyond Borders* delves into the importance and benefits of friendship, reminding the reader of its positive effect on health and longevity, describing gender differences, and commenting on the recent impact of social media on friendship networks. The book connects all the dots, presenting opposing views and explaining complexities in a clear and engaging manner.

While *Friends Beyond Borders* describes the joys and excitement friendships beyond borders can bring, it doesn't whitewash intercultural friendships. It clearly delineates why they can be difficult and sometimes disappointing. In a recent study I conducted with international students in the United States, an Asian student ruminated that his low English proficiency, cultural differences, and also a perceived lack of interest on the part of Americans resulted in his having no American friends a year into his sojourn. This student's comment that "Americans don't need Asian male friends" bespeaks of loneliness and missed opportunities on both sides.

Friends Beyond Borders is a call to reach out, to broaden one's horizon and form friendships that cross borders. The passion with which Baumgarte makes this call entices readers to embark on the adventure.

Elisabeth Gareis
Professor
April 2013, Tarrytown, NY

Chapter 1

How it all started

America is my country and Paris is my hometown.

–Gertrude Stein

I began my professional life as a nerd. My doctoral dissertation was about retrieval processes in long-term memory, esoteric stuff that always left me conversationally impaired whenever someone would ask about it. I loved this research, but seldom succeeded in getting others to share my enthusiasm. If I talked about it at all, my excitement was met with vacant stares, droopy eyelids, or furtive glances elsewhere, anywhere, in search of more interesting conversational territory.

I wasn't a big hit at cocktail parties.

I was a bigger hit with my employer, Winthrop University, since that research led to significant publications in leading journals. I exploited that little niche, doing my research, teaching my courses, which earned me advancements and promotions, eventually to the level of full professor. The best part, in 1988, midway through my career, I was awarded a yearlong sabbatical teaching at the American University in Paris. My year in Paris turned out to be life changing.

There I was, 41 years old, having traveled abroad only twice before, and those were just short vacations, doing touristy things, never staying long in one spot, just having fun taking in the sights. This time would be entirely different. I was not simply going as an observer, but actually to "live" abroad. My teaching duties at the American University were quite modest, and as a visiting professor, I had no committee or other administrative responsibilities. So I would have time for a rich cultural experience.

Through a friend of a colleague, I secured a small one-bedroom, fourth floor walk-up flat near Place St. Michel, in the heart of the Latin Quarter of Paris. It was about as culturally distant from Winthrop and small town South Carolina as I could get. My apartment was sunny and quiet, facing a tiny inner courtyard, although a constant carnival of young partiers and tourists awaited me nearly any time of the day or night, the moment I exited the massive, squeaky front door of the building.

I'm not a teacher: only a fellow-traveler of whom you asked the way. I pointed ahead - ahead of myself as well as you.

–George Bernard Shaw

I had completed a six-week intensive French language-training program just prior to my arrival. Even so, my language skills were minimal. I was able to explain I was there for "une année sabbatique" although any response I received always left me speechless. I was determined to make the most of my year abroad. The large expat community in Paris was very welcoming, but after fifteen years in small town South Carolina, I was intent on meeting French people and having a genuinely French "année sabbatique."

Those who know nothing of foreign languages know nothing of their own.

–Johann Wolfgang von Goethe

The American University in Paris provided me with continued language training and I devoted a lot of energy to the boring tasks of memorizing vocabulary and conjugating verbs. Language is such an intrinsically social phenomenon—after all, it was invented to help us humans communicate with each other. Yet learning to speak a foreign language requires hours and hours of solitary drudgery. Frankly, I was lonesome. I wanted someone to talk to, other than my practice recordings.

I have always devoted a lot of energy to my friendships. I was married and divorced early, and remained single through most of my adult life until meeting my current wife, Susan, when I was in my late forties. To compensate for not having a life partner for so long, I naturally cultivated close friendships. So, I missed my friends a lot during my first weeks in Paris, and I wanted desperately to make new ones, to make French friends.

I cringe to think about all my early, futile attempts to make new friends in Paris. At that time, there were no internet-based social media to facilitate meeting like-minded people. So I would boldly—and often quite clumsily—try to strike up conversations with total strangers in the open-air markets, in cafés, anywhere I sensed an opportunity in my day-to-day life. I was eager to try out my French on anyone willing to converse with me. But people simply didn't have the time or the patience to deal with my bumbling and babbling.

> *To be alone is to be different, to be different is to be alone.*
>
> –Suzanne Gordon

Then I made an interesting discovery.

A new strategy

The French people I encountered were always quite polite, and I learned this *politesse* carried certain norms and expectations regarding appropriate behavior once one enters into a conversation. Combine that idea with the fact that the French have all been thoroughly schooled— more like indoctrinated—in the proper use of their language, so much so they often feel compelled to correct linguistic errors made by foreigners. Even total strangers would sometimes volunteer to correct how I was saying something.

> *In Paris they just simply opened their eyes and stared when we spoke to them in French! We never did succeed in making those idiots understand their own language.*
>
> –Mark Twain

I soon developed a deliberate tactic for exploiting these occurrences. Whenever a stranger corrected something I had just said, I discovered that as long as I used the polite, elevated language appropriate for the situation, I could keep them in conversation for an eternity. And I did! I would ask questions about the error, seek clarification, lament my futile attempts to learn their language, ask whether they had ever been to the U.S., and on, and on, and on. My little routine grew almost comical, but it worked. Since they initiated the conversation, and I was being socially appropriate, politeness obligated them to stick with me until I turned them loose. It was such great fun!

Unfortunately, I never managed to convert even one of these exchanges into anything beyond a momentary touch of humanity. My loneliness egged me on.

Plan B

Several language schools in my Parisian neighborhood specialized in teaching English, and one of them had a public bulletin board where students would place ads for babysitting, flats, pets, and things of this nature. I posted an ad seeking a language exchange with someone whose English was about at the level of my French, a half-hour of English conversation for a half-hour of French. I wrote the ad in French, and I suspect it demonstrated the feeble level of my expertise in their language.

> If you talk to a man in a language he understands, that goes to his head. If you talk to him in his language, that goes to his heart.
>
> -Nelson Mandela

The response was overwhelming. My phone wouldn't stop ringing. I may have received 40 calls before I managed to get by the school and remove the ad. I followed up only four of the contacts, meeting with them often, usually in cafés where the strong espresso seemed to have beneficial effects on both my desire and ability to speak French.

Becoming friends

I hold the fondest memories of those conversations—they were exhilarating and magical! For each meeting, I would prepare the vocabulary to discuss what was going on in my life that week, a novel I was reading, events in the news, or something about French culture. As our language skills developed, so did the breadth and depth of our conversations. There is something about struggling to communicate with another human being, each with limited linguistic skills in the other's language that sets the stage for developing a friendship.

We intended to share our languages but ended up sharing our lives, our hopes, our joys as well as our challenges and disappointments. These four individuals made my year in Paris a transformative experience, although I didn't even begin to appreciate this fact at the time.

I was simply having fun, enjoying my sabbatical to the fullest, even up to the very last minute. I did learn to communicate comfortably in French, and I participated in French cultural life as I had set out to do the day I arrived. Of course, I was not French and didn't want to be French. In fact, I seemed to appreciate and value my American cultural roots even more after spending a year away from my homeland.

As much as I was enjoying my bohemian life in Paris, I genuinely looked forward to my return. I was ready to be living in my own house, to shower in my own bathroom, to drive my own car, to reconnect with my work, my colleagues, my students, and most of all my friends whom I missed. I had so many stories to tell!

Rude awakenings

But reality hit hard! Despite my longings and anticipation, my homecoming was by far the most difficult aspect of my sabbatical. I know now I suffered from something cross-cultural experts refer to as "reentry shock," a kind of culture shock in reverse, where returning to one's home culture generates discomfort because one has become unconsciously accustomed to living with a new set of social norms and expectations. The feelings are hard to describe, but I felt out of place, like I didn't belong. Nothing seemed quite right, but I couldn't explain why. I especially noticed this around my friends and favorite work colleagues.

Remember that happiness is a way of travel, not a destination.

–Roy Goodman

While they were genuinely enthused to see me, and I them, there seemed to be a kind of disjointedness in our relationships. For one thing, I had all of these stories to tell and their attention span for them seemed unduly limited. I wanted to reconnect so badly, yet I found their responses to my overtures unsatisfying.

At the time, it was difficult to explain the feelings I had. In fact, I saw my friends often, talking, laughing, doing things together, sharing our lives as we had always done in the past. But something was missing, and I was at a loss to explain what that was.

Confusion

These feelings of disjointedness seemed to last, and I became obsessed with trying to understand what was going on. My social life seemed unnatural, awkward and uncomfortable, especially with close friends and work colleagues. I found it difficult to talk with anyone about it for fear of sounding like I was accusing my friends of not being there for me, as if they were doing something wrong or offensive.

In fact, it was I who had changed.

I noticed some disjointedness in other parts of my life, and as any inquisitive-minded psychologist would do, I began to read the literature on people who have moved from one culture to the next and suffered from culture shock. I suspected I was suffering from the consequences of shifting cultures. One thing was clear. I had looked forward to and was quite happy being back home. I was ready and eager to re-establish my life, both professionally and personally. But I also realized I had changed in some fundamental ways and these changes caused me discomfort, especially in my relationships with my closest friends.

Not everything that is faced can be changed, but nothing can be changed until it is faced.

-James Baldwin

New beginnings

To telegraph my story, these experiences returning home from Paris in 1989 were so striking that within three months after my return, I decided to abandon my comfortable academic research niche in cognition and memory. I was going to examine friendships as my new field of research. Specifically, I decided to investigate cultural variations in close friendships.

There is one thing stronger than all the armies in the world; and that is an idea whose time has come.

-Victor Hugo

Even today, decades later, I get a lump in my throat and chills down my spine just thinking about what a major turning point that was in my life. This kind of thing simply isn't done in academia. It's a bit like divorcing your family and trying to join a new one. The lack of graduate training and the mentoring and professional connections such training provides meant I would always be something of an outsider in my new field.

On the upside, I had already earned tenure, I was well-respected as a teacher of my college courses, and so it was unlikely I would be risking my employment. Most importantly, I was committed, truly committed to developing a deeper understanding of how close friendships differ in other cultures and sharing my findings with others. Nothing would stop me!

It is now over 20 years later, I'm retired from academia and *Friends Beyond Borders* represents what I have learned in the interim. This book is partly a memoir about my personal experiences with close friends abroad and in the U.S., and partly a research report about my quest to learn all I could about the nature of cultural differences in close friendships, especially how friendships in the U.S. differ from those in other countries.

Broadening my cultural horizons

My new area of research led to some other major changes in my life, such as developing and teaching a course in cross-cultural psychology. But it wasn't long after I began my reading about the cultural aspects of social behaviors when

You cannot create experience. You must undergo it.

–Albert Camus

I realized that, in the eyes of cross-cultural experts and the ways they have of measuring these things, the U.S. and France are not terrifically different. If I wanted to get serious about studying cultural differences in close friendships and extend my research and personal experiences to a wider variety of situations, I would need to spend time in a much more divergent culture. I started applying for opportunities that would allow me to spend another year abroad, this time focusing more on Asian and African cultures.

In 1994, I was hired for one year by the University of Maryland to teach psychology courses on U.S. military bases in South Korea. I lived off base, in a relatively small town just south of Seoul and although my teaching responsibilities were rather demanding, I still found time to learn some of the language and to engage in a rich social life among Koreans not associated with the U.S. military. By this time, I was already administering surveys and asking people lots of questions about their closest friendships.

Because of these personal sojourns in France and South Korea, many of the anecdotes I use to illustrate my findings are derived from these two cultures, comparing friendships there to those in the U.S. My data include other cultures as well, having surveyed and interviewed international students studying in the U.S. coming from thirteen different countries. I developed surveys in five other languages permitting me to collect data within China, Cuba, Spain, and Romania, in addition to the U.S., France and South Korea. These results have allowed me to see a wide variety of approaches to friendship.

The best interviews — like the best biographies — should sing the strangeness and variety of the human race.

-Lynn Barber

The fact is people have very different notions about what it means to be a good friend. Some of these differences are a matter of personal preferences or one's unique personality. But some are the result of one's cultural background. I hope to provide some insight and understanding about the cultural influences on how we think about and feel about our closest friends.

To you, the reader

Friends Beyond Borders is intended for all those who value their close friendships as I do. It is especially aimed at those who have experienced a major cultural shift at some point in their lives and were left with questions or disappointments in their social lives. I also hope to have something to offer those of you who are simply interested in broadening your social and cultural horizons. With our ever-increasing global community, you don't need to travel abroad to experience a new culture. You may find it living next door, or simply a click away on the Internet.

Whenever I talk about my research to anyone who has ventured across cultural lines, often there is an instant excitement and heartfelt recognition of what I am talking about. This is especially true for people who have moved to the U.S. from abroad. *Friends Beyond Borders* explains to newcomers how people in the U.S. tend to think and feel about their closest friends. It will also help those born in the U.S.

understand and appreciate other approaches to friendship and how these friendships can be enormously enriching and satisfying.

I will be discussing six styles of close friendship that vary systematically across cultures, and in each case, I'll be contrasting how friendships are typically conceived in the U.S. with those in other cultures. It is also true one can find very clear examples of all six styles of friendship right here in the U.S., a result of our long history of immigration from a wide range of cultures. Even within a culture, it is natural for people to adopt differing ideas about what it means to be a close friend. These differing assumptions can lead to miscommunications and misunderstandings, even among people with purely friendly intentions. My aim is to clarify these differing notions about what it means to be a good friend.

The better part of one's life consists of his friendships.

-Abraham Lincoln

My ultimate goal is to encourage friendships that reach across borders. I'm especially interested in cultural borders, but later on, I'll explore gender boundaries as well, how men and women might differ in their approaches to friendship. I will also devote an entire chapter to the benefits, especially the health benefits of close friendships of all kinds. And a book on friendship would not be complete without looking at ways that the computer and the Internet have influenced how we socialize.

Regardless of your preferred style of friendship, I hope this book will help you think of your close friendships in new and creative ways.

Chapter 2

What is friendship?

The best things in life aren't things.

–Art Buchwald

Who do you consider to be your very best friend?

I encourage you to take a moment and consider this question carefully. Why do you consider this person to be your best friend? Is it because you've known him or her longer than anyone else? Is it because this person came forward to help you out in a particularly difficult period in your life? Or is it simply because you enjoy this person's company the most? Maybe it's the easy laughter and enjoyable conversations whenever you are together?

Some of us might have a tough time coming up with just one person we think of as our closest friend. Perhaps we think of a small number of people as being our closest friends, despite the grammatical stricture that there can be only one "best" or "closest" friend. This small number of very special people in our lives might vary slightly from year to year, as people move to new locations, get married or divorced, or simply drift apart.

More than a playmate

I would like you to keep your best friend, or this small number of closest friends, in mind throughout this book. *Friends Beyond Borders* is about them and your relationships with them. As you read on, you will notice I often use the expression "close friends" implying that I am not talking about friends as the term is often loosely used in English. In everyday speech, we might say something like, "I want you to meet my friend Leslie," and Leslie could be someone I just met at a conference, for example.

When I speak of friendship, I am referring to just those whom you consider your closest friends, where the basis of the relationship grows out of mutual concern and affection more than some common interest or activity. We all have tennis friends, friends at work or friends in our neighborhood. In my definition, a close friendship is one that extends beyond these built-in commonalities, one that has endured changes in geography or life roles, such as getting married or changing jobs. You've remained friends despite these changes in life circumstances.

Friendship is the hardest thing in the world to explain. It's not something you learn in school. But if you haven't learned the meaning of friendship, you really haven't learned anything.

–Muhammad Ali

By contrast, Dale Carnegie's classic 1936 book *How to Win Friends and Influence People* is not about friendship as I use the term here. Carnegie's book, as interesting and valuable as it is, talks more about the advantages of being friendly than it does about close friendships. Friendliness is a personality characteristic, not a relationship, not the same as having close friends. His ideas encourage one to bring a friendly demeanor to work settings in order to enhance one's social influence and personal success. He says little about cultivating close relationships for their intrinsic value and enjoyment, which is the true meaning of friendship.

Friends Beyond Borders primarily concerns how people in various cultures think about, feel about, and behave toward their closest friends, and how this contrasts with friendships in the U.S. What I have learned over the past 20 years is that people in different cultures can have very incompatible notions about what it means to be a good friend. What one person sees as a friendly gesture, another could see as downright insulting.

Perhaps you have lived among people in a culture different from yours, and you've had first-hand experiences of what I am talking about. Some have even argued that men and women have different cultural orientations when it comes to close relationships. My hope is to clarify these differing and often contradictory ideas about close friendship.

Getting started

It is also worth looking at how professionals who study these relationships—researchers in psychology, sociology or communications—define the term friendship. (Sources for all work presented in this book can be found at www.friendsbeyondbordersbook.com.) *The beginning of wisdom* These researchers are obsessed with *is a definition of terms.* defining how critical terms are employed in their fields of endeavor and when I put on —Socrates my research hat, I am no exception. Interestingly, my technical or professional definition of friendship evolved significantly over the years, as I learned more about how other cultures view these relationships. In fact, defining the concept of friendship has turned out to be an ongoing adventure in developing cultural awareness. Taking you through a bit of this evolution will provide a sneak preview of the many cultural influences on friendship and will set the stage for the rest of the book.

It was true in 1989 when I began my research, and it is still true to a great extent today, that social researchers in the U.S., other English speaking countries, and Western Europe dominate the systematic study of close relationships. I've come to realize their definitions of friendship betray their cultural biases in many critical ways. I'll give you just three examples.

The chosen ones

All of these researchers view friendship as a *voluntary* relationship. Unlike family relationships, they hold, one chooses one's friends and the maintenance of these relationships is entirely a matter of personal choice. We can decide to stop being friends with someone, and there is little to keep us from breaking off the relationship. It is seen as a choice we can exercise at any point in time.

Most experts consider this voluntary aspect to be a uniquely defining characteristic of friendship. They view even romantic relationships as not completely voluntary, as echoed in such expressions as "falling in love" or "love at first sight" or by the fact that, in some cultures, marriages are to varying degrees arranged by family members.

It came as a revelation early on when I discovered that many cultures of the world do not see friendship as entirely voluntary, as we do. For example in East Asian cultures such as China or Korea, there is the strong belief that one's friendships are a matter of fate. My Korean friends are forever telling me we were predestined to be good friends. For them, friendship is not a matter of personal choice. As a result, they think of their friendship experiences, good and bad, as something that must be accepted, celebrated in the good times, but simply tolerated at other times. Friendships are something over which they feel very little control.

Friends among equals

The biases of Western social researchers show up in other aspects of their definition of friendship. All of them, without exception, see friendship as based on an assumption of equality. Friends are assumed to be equal or similar in all outward respects—a wide variation in age, education or socioeconomic background would be considered exceptions to the rule, and would have to be dealt with in some fashion to produce at least the semblance of equality. Friends with widely differing ages could consider the older friend as "young at heart" for example.

This assumption of equality within a friendship would not apply to many cultures of the world. For these cultures, all social relationships have, by nature, a hierarchical structure to them. Some cultures even have different terms for an older friend versus a younger friend. This age difference, even when quite small, carries implications about power, responsibility and deference. The older friend, like an older brother or sister, can dominate the relationship in critical ways and at the same time, would feel a sense of duty to take care of the younger "sibling." These notions simply don't fit with the presumption that friendship is a relationship between equals.

Friends as VIPs

Most Western social scientists see friendship as implying priority—one selects certain people to be friends, while others are not considered in this exclusive category. Our close friends are a select group who are very important in our lives.

Again, this concept of priority would not fit the definition of friendship in many cultures of the world. In some African cultures, for example, family ties are so strong and important that friendships, while highly valued, carry a much lower status by comparison. In Nigeria, one could call a friend a "brother," but one would never call a brother a "friend" since that would be denigrating this important family relationship.

Each friend represents a world in us, a world not born until they arrive, and it is only by this meeting that a new world is born.

–Anais Nin

There are a number of other ways in which simply defining the term friendship produces a myriad of cultural complications. I've taken you through these problems with definitions simply to make the point that, from a cross-cultural perspective, even coming up with a standard definition of "friendship" that would apply in all cases is next to impossible. We each have very different ideas about what it means to be a good friend.

Yet most people wouldn't even consider such a thing possible—we assume friendships are the same the world over. It isn't until we spend a significant period of our lives in another culture that we come to realize not everyone thinks of friendship the way we do. Friendships that cross cultural lines can be very enlightening and fulfilling, but they can also be quite confusing. It is my goal with this book to alleviate this confusion.

Not waxing poetic

In conducting my research, I allowed the men and women who participated in my surveys and interviews to use their own criteria to determine whom they considered their closest friends. On the surveys, I simply asked them to choose one person from among their closest friends to be the focus of the many questions I posed. The answers I received provide a rich tapestry of the many versions of close friendship that exist in the world.

If you are not accustomed to a scientific approach to such things as close relationships, it might be helpful to clarify what this book is and what it isn't. *Friends Beyond Borders* is clearly not an emotion-laden, poetic ode to the lofty beauties and merits of close friendship.

While I occasionally have these thoughts and feelings about my own close friends, this book takes a very different approach. In the tradition of empirical social research, I have collected survey data and conducted interviews with volunteers in a number of widely different cultures. I've analyzed these data with a variety of techniques intended to tease out how people differ in their thinking about close friendships.

In the sweetness of friendship let there be laughter, and sharing of pleasures. For in the dew of little things the heart finds its morning and is refreshed.

-Kahlil Gibran

Most of what I will explain is based on this kind of research, my own and that of many others; but I promise not to bore you with statistics or pie charts. My findings can be readily seen in the everyday lives of the people who have shared their friendship stories with me. Having lived for extended periods of time in France and South Korea, I'm especially interested in how friendships in the U.S. differ from those in these two cultures, and I've included my own personal stories and those of others to illustrate these differences.

Friendships under the microscope

I'm fully aware a scientific approach to understanding something as personal and individually unique as friendship might raise doubts in the eyes of many. I can appreciate such skepticism. As a person who values his friendships at many different levels, I must confess to some inner conflict about applying scientific methods to such a delicate matter as our close relationships. The fact is, we who work in this field attempt to reduce our thoughts, feelings, motives, and the many other complexities of close friendships into a set of numbers on a spreadsheet. It can all seem rather dehumanizing. Many would see it as a patently artificial way of examining human nature.

Experts often possess more data than judgment.

-Colin Powell

I have tens of thousands of data points reflecting each response of each participant on some survey question measuring how they think about a close friend. I've sliced and diced and categorized people's friendships with the aim of providing some insights into the role culture and gender play in these intensely individual and personal experiences.

The benefits are real

I will be the first to admit such statistical abstractions are only a distant echo of the lived experience of close friendship. However, I encourage you to keep an open mind about this way of analyzing and understanding close friendships. In my own life, years of number crunching have brought me to some life-changing realizations about the nature of my personal friendships. I hope the same for you.

Recall from Chapter One I delved into this line of research after returning from my first year abroad feeling bewildered and perplexed about my friendships at home in the U.S. I now have a much better understanding of what that was all about, which has only served to deepen my affections for all my friends.

In this book, I'll be talking about six different styles of close friendship, and later on, the role that gender and social media play in these relationships. I see these different versions of friendship playing out all around me, among my personal friends, and among the friends of those who populate my everyday life. I appreciate my friends more because I recognize the wide range of ways friendships can be expressed.

I don't think I'm alone in finding the implications of this line of research meaningful. When I present these ideas in public forums, I often get feedback from audience members who feel they have gained important insights into their friendships, clarifying aspects that have troubled them in the past. This is especially true for individuals who have extensive experience with a culture other than the one where they grew up. They see their friendships in a new light, realizing they have never fully understood or appreciated their friends' intentions before. There is a sense of renewed energy and enthusiasm for their friends. This kind of feedback is deeply rewarding—marking the best days of my life!

So much left to do

I've developed and administered thousands of surveys and conducted confidential interviews since the early '90s, but even so, my data sets are modest compared to those of so many others in the field of cross-cultural research. We researchers are a cautious lot, so in a spirit of prudence, my conclusions should be seen as tentative at this point. My hope is this work will encourage other researchers to do a more thorough and comprehensive job of what I have begun. Perhaps they will find the study of close friendships as interesting and fulfilling as I have, to push our understanding of these phenomena far beyond these beginnings.

The purpose of computing is insight, not numbers.

-Richard W. Hamming

Regardless of the value of my contributions to this field, I think discussing our different approaches to friendship is a conversation worth having, and I offer this book, the first of its kind aimed at a general audience, as an attempt to broach the subject directly and empirically. Ultimately, of course, you as the reader get to judge the utility of these concepts.

Looking ahead

By way of an overview, Chapters Four through Ten examine in depth the six different cultural styles of close friendship, which are summarized in the table on the next page. In each case, the style of friendship most common in the U.S. (on the right side in the table) is contrasted with a style that can be documented in certain other cultures.

In Chapter Eleven, I lay out a broad array of findings to show that cultivating close friendships can be very good for your health and wellbeing. This is intended to encourage friendships of all sorts, whether or not they cross cultural or gender borders. Chapter Twelve looks at gender specifically, calling into question whether men and women are truly from different planets when it comes to how they deal with their close friends. Chapter Thirteen looks at social media, especially Facebook, and attempts to answer the question of what it has to do with friendship. Finally, Chapter Fourteen ties it all together.

I begin our discussion in Chapter Three with a look at what researchers and theorists in the field had to say about cultural differences in close friendships beginning at the point I first started this research. I learned early on the U.S. stands out from most cultures of the world with regard to the issue of close friendships, but not in ways I ever would have guessed.

The six cultural styles of close friendship

Interveners

They see it as their duty to take care of their friends, to instruct, advise, aid and protect them, even intervening in each other's lives when appropriate.

Independents

They show affection for their friends by making time for them, enjoying their company, but also by providing words of encouragement during difficult times.

Excluders

They make clear distinctions in their behaviors, emotions, and thinking between close friends and those who are simply acquaintances.

Includers

They are outwardly friendly toward everyone, distinguishing between friends and acquaintances only in their thoughts and feelings.

Realists

They think of their closest friends very objectively, seeing both their good and not-so-good characteristics. Their talk tends to be frank and straightforward.

Idealists

They think of their closest friends in very idealized terms, and strive to always be upbeat and positive in their friendship interactions.

Chapter 3

What the experts have to say

There is a scarcity of friendship, but not of friends.

–Thomas Fuller

Did you know we in the U.S. have a bad reputation, internationally speaking, when it comes to the issue of close friendship? This little factoid came as a big surprise to me when I first began reading about cultural differences in close friendship, my new field of research. Believe it or not, most other cultures see us as shallow and uncommitted, even in our closest friendships.

This notion is quite pervasive, and has been in circulation for well over a century and a half. As far as I can tell, it all began with the writings of Alexis de Tocqueville back in 1831, with his grand treatise, *Democracy in America*. In this oft-cited tome, he described people in the U.S. as restless, competitively striving for the good life, with the result that ties between individuals were characteristically transient and casual. He concluded that people in the U.S. were open and friendly, but their strong sense of individualism and interpersonal competitiveness didn't allow for deep and committed friendships.

De Tocqueville's words became a sort of troubling refrain for all my readings those first few months. Professionals from a wide variety of backgrounds, cross-cultural psychologists, sociologists, anthropologists, experts in communications, even books written for business personnel preparing for an overseas assignment were all saying the same thing: Americans, when compared to people from other cultures, were less interested in close, committed friendships. We are typically described as open and friendly, just not good candidates for the kinds of friendships others see as the norm.

Which Americans?

Speaking of Americans, what does that term mean exactly? Before going on, I'd like to take a moment to discuss a quandary faced by cross-cultural researchers of every persuasion, and that is, how to label people who live in the U.S. Of course, we are typically referred to as "Americans," but that label poses problems when making comparisons across cultures. Strictly speaking, the term "Americans" includes Canadians, as well as Central and South Americans. In fact, all of us on the American continents could be labeled Americans. In the context of cross-cultural work, it is potentially confusing to infer Americans are only those who live in the United States.

All other countries have a unique noun to refer to their peoples, the French, Chinese, , etc. People in the U.S. are lacking such a distinctive label. So I have taken the liberty of borrowing a term I've seen in blogs coming out of the U.K. They refer to people in the U.S. as USAers.

In typing this term, it's already clear my word processing software doesn't recognize it as an established word in the vast English lexicon. I've searched it on Google and found it used nowhere other than those blogs I mentioned. It can't be found in even the largest dictionaries. As a term, I think it is available, and for the sake of clarity, I will be using it to refer to "people in the U.S." from now on.

I know by inventing such a term, I risk the ire of many for whom the term "American" is sacred and to mess with it would be civic apostasy. I feel a strong attachment to this country and its heritage, and in my defense, I would argue it is entirely appropriate to use the term "American" when saluting the flag or singing patriotic anthems.

However, in this context, where I will be making frequent comparisons across cultures, it is better to avoid ambiguity and make the point we USAers are not the only occupants of this continent. By the way, I pronounce the term as "you-SAY-ers" although you should feel free to pronounce it anyway you like.

Everyone agrees, USAers are superficial

Getting back to what I was learning in those first months in my new field of research, I quickly grew to appreciate that we USAers are not seen internationally as being interested in true friendship to the extent others are. Robert Bellah and coauthors in their influential book, *Habits of the Heart*, suggested that not only do USAers favor superficial friendships, they resist being too strongly attached to family members as well, since such obligations and entanglements can restrain their personal freedoms.

USAers have valued this sense of personal freedom since the days of the early settlers who left Europe in search of greater personal, religious and social liberty. They also came to make a lot of money. According to Bellah and colleagues, being tied down with close friends or even family members can infringe on both one's personal freedoms and the preoccupation with making a good living. They asserted that the primary function of friendship among USAers was the enjoyment of each other's company, and not much beyond that.

Edward Stewart, an anthropologist, similarly argued USAers use the term "friend" quite loosely, to refer to anyone from a life-long soul mate to someone recently encountered at a party. USAers are

> *We are all in this together, by ourselves.*
>
> –Lily Tomlin

doers, he claimed, always busy with work, play, sports and hobbies, and they have a separate set of friends for each of these activities, "compartmentalized" as he referred to it. So we have our tennis friends, our college friends, our work friends, each group neatly confined to its own social compartment. Like others, he concluded that USAers tend to be quite warm, open, and friendly, but that close and committed friendships are relatively rare.

Lots of questions

All these experts left me wondering if the differences I experienced between my friendships in France and those at home, the issue that started me down this path of inquiry in the first place, could simply be explained as a matter of depth? Are we just shallower with our friends here in the U.S? Are we too preoccupied with success and ourselves to cultivate deep and enduring friendships?

Some aspects of what I was reading did ring true to me. For example, I agree with the assertion USAers are characteristically friendly. The average USAer walking down the street, even a New Yorker, tends to be friendlier than the average Parisian, at least in my experience. We smile a lot, even when speaking to perfect strangers. I often noticed this fact when observing USAer tourists interacting with French people in Paris. We value being open and friendly, we expect others to be the same, and we are disappointed and critical when they are not.

There is nothing the matter with Americans except their ideals. The real American is all right; it is the ideal American who is all wrong.

–G.K. Chesterton

But are we a shallow lot, especially when it comes to our closest friendships? I had difficulty accepting that idea. I felt then, and still feel today, that USAers have very close and fulfilling friendships.

USAer self perceptions

I discussed this issue on several occasions with my associates in the psychology department and other colleagues on campus, especially those who had lived for a period of time in other cultures, and the responses I got were surprisingly consistent. Most of them agreed, when compared to other cultures, USAers tend to have shallower friendships. However, without exception, they all asserted that this generalized USAer stereotype didn't apply to them personally, that they were the exceptions to the rule, that their friendships were genuine and meaningful relationships. Each claimed to have good friends who would stand by them through thick or thin.

The consistency of their responses left me wondering whether this notion that USAers relegate themselves to only superficial friendships might simply be a collective mythology about our national character.

I knew my friendships in the U.S. contrasted significantly with those I had recently made in France, but simply explaining this difference as a matter of depth or commitment seemed misleading or at the least, unsatisfying. When it came to knowing my friends well, for example, I certainly knew my USAer friends for a longer period of time and in much greater depth and detail compared to my French friends.

I felt free to talk about anything with my USAer friends, even the most delicate or personal issues. I don't think I felt a similar freedom with my French friends. What I would eventually learn is that cultures differ, not only in terms of how they conduct their friendships, but also in the ways they define closeness and intimacy in a relationship. In subsequent chapters, I will argue USAers do cultivate close, meaningful friendships, but definitions of closeness vary significantly over cultures.

The standardized American is largely a myth created not least by Americans themselves.

–Irwin Edman

As an aside, I should acknowledge the risk of using my own personal experiences as the basis for understanding cultural differences in close friendships. I always consider the possibility that the contrast I perceive in my close friendships here and abroad may stem from the fact that my friends in other cultures treat me differently simply because I am a USAer. To them, I can be a novel and interesting experience, something different from their norm. Perhaps they aren't showing me their typical friendship behaviors. Clearly, they are often fascinated by the ways in which I do and don't fulfill their stereotype of a typical USAer.

So while I use my own personal experiences extensively throughout this book by way of examples, I fully appreciate that only objective, systematic research can provide meaningful answers to the questions those experiences have raised.

But claiming USAers are more superficial in their friendships seemed, at the very least, an overly simplistic explanation. Like my colleagues, I didn't feel this description applied to my USAer friendships. USAers in general seemed to need and want close friendship as much as anyone—isn't that part of being human? These thoughts inspired me to find more satisfying explanations for these questions.

Relationship researchers

At this point in my reading I discovered the field of "relationship research," whose definition of friendship and its cultural biases I described in Chapter Two. Since my previous research focused entirely on cognition and memory, I had only a passing awareness of this field of study and its major findings. These scholars conduct empirical research and create fascinating theories about all sorts of relationships, especially romantic or marital relationships, friendships, and family relationships.

I soon discovered there were two professional organizations representing this field, each with its own leadership, meetings and journal. Nearly every relationship researcher I met those first years belonged to both groups. To my amusement, I learned these two organizations used to be a single society that split because different factions couldn't get along. Apparently their professional expertise in close relationships wasn't sufficient to help them get past their interpersonal conflicts.

An apology is the superglue of life. It can repair just about anything.

–Lynn Johnston

In recent years, these two factions have reconciled and merged into a single organization called the International Association for Relationship Research (IARR)—my faith in relationship researchers has been restored!

An omission worth exploring

Perusing their journals, I found relatively few studies were done on friendship compared to romantic or family relationships. Even so, there were hundreds of research reports, which investigated any and every aspect of friendship you could imagine, from theoretical underpinnings, to friendship formation, to gender differences, to self-disclosure patterns, including even the dissolution of friendships.

The worst solitude is to be destitute of sincere friendship.

–Francis Bacon

One thing I learned from these and other such sources is nearly all friendship studies were conducted in the U.S. or Canada, and even when studies were done outside these two countries, they rarely examined differences across cultural boundaries. When I first began my research, cultural differences in our social behaviors rarely interested relationship researchers. By contrast, today perhaps a third or a half of the articles in current issues of their journals include culture as a variable under investigation. Relationship researchers have grown passionate in their search to understand cultural differences in how we conduct our personal relationships.

But when I began I was disappointed to find so little to satisfy my curiosity. This void was also an opportunity needing attention and I was enthusiastically committed to giving it the effort it deserved.

Cross-cultural research

I then examined the cross-cultural literature in psychology and communications and found a great deal written about cultural influences on our social habits. Surprisingly, many of these writings were aimed at the business community, since large corporations were quickly "going international" in the early '90s, and as a result, they were grappling with cultural matters that greatly complicated personnel issues at every level of their organizations. These early multinationals also provided a readily available pool of research participants, all of whom had similar education, training and background, but differed only in their geography and cultures. Some of the most influential studies of the time compared the cultural values of workers of the same multinational corporation drawn from their many affiliates around the globe.

I learned that cross-cultural researchers had developed very clever ways of measuring and categorizing cultures based on these large-scale studies. They measured such things as the extent to which people respected authorities, how closely a culture ran on time, the degree to which people believed in fate or destiny, or the value people placed on relationships.

The results were a kind of cultural profile for each country, somewhat like a scientifically derived stereotype of the typical person in each culture. I found this stuff endlessly fascinating; especially comparing the profiles of the two cultures I knew best, the U.S. and France. I should quickly add that all researchers cautioned adamantly against over-generalizing these stereotypes. One can never assume that a particular individual has any resemblance to their national stereotype, even if it is based on tens of thousands of research participants.

A core dimension

One of these cultural dimensions that showed up in every researcher's lexicon in various forms was individualism versus collectivism, and it has served as a jumping off point for my own studies of friendship as well. It is worth spending a few moments describing this dimension in some detail.

Individualist cultures are ones where the emphasis is on the individual as the basic unit of society. Even young children in these societies are raised to develop their own individual personalities, their own personhoods. They are encouraged to assert themselves, to express their own opinions, to make their own decisions, and to be responsible for themselves. A concept like fairness would be thought of in terms of one's own individual rights. A lot of emphasis is placed on developing a healthy identity and positive self-esteem. Perhaps you have already guessed: USAers tend to score very high on this dimension.

Happiness is having a large, loving, caring, close-knit family in another city.

–George Burns

In collectivist cultures, by contrast, the family is thought of as the basic unit of society. One's identity is tied inextricably to that of the family. One would think of one's self as a mother or father, son or daughter, brother or sister, more than as a person with particular needs and goals independent of the family. In collectivist societies, family members feel responsible for each another. Everything one does reflects on other members of the family as well. If a child or an adult succeeds, the entire family feels this success; if he or she fails, the entire family feels shame, and these connections persist all the way through one's life.

There is often a tendency toward authoritarianism in collectivist cultures, where older members of the family, usually the father or grandfather, make major decisions for everyone else. Individuals are loyal to their families and in return, families protect and take care of them, in every respect, emotionally, physically, and economically.

Data relevant to this dimension have been gathered on all major cultures of the world by different researchers using a variety of methods. While there are minor variations, their findings tend to be strikingly similar. The U.S. and other English-speaking cultures tend to score highest on individualism, followed closely by Western and Northern European countries. The remaining cultures on the planet score to varying degrees toward the collectivist end of the spectrum. The most collectivist cultures seem to be in Central and South America, East Asia and Africa.

Some of the most astute observations about the individualism-collectivism dimension and its manifestations in our everyday social lives were written by Harry Triandis, Geert Hofstede, Edward T. Hall, and Bill Gudykunst who, I quickly learned, were the elder statesmen of cross-cultural research.

USAers and friendship

What did these experts have to say about friendship and culture? When USAers, often seen as the quintessential individualists, are compared to other, more collectivist cultures, the conclusion often drawn is reminiscent of that of de Tocqueville over a century and a half ago: USAers are generally quite warm, friendly, and approachable, they conclude, but deep, committed and involved friendships are not highly valued.

Even when the experts all agree, they may well be mistaken.

–Bertrand Russell

The explanation of their conclusion also paralleled that of de Tocqueville. They made much out of the idea that USAers value their personal freedom, their ability to make their own choices, even in trivial day-to-day matters. For the typical USAer, they argued, having very close and committed friendships complicates this need. It means they would have to give up some personal control. Close friendships require compromising. Whenever friends are together, they must negotiate what they will do or how they will do it, and at least one among them will not be getting first choice. According to these experts, such sacrifices in the name of friendship are not attractive for USAers.

In their view, USAers try to avoid these choices, by having friends that coincide with their interests or activities, as suggested by the "compartmentalized" friendships described by Edward Stewart. But the overriding philosophy seems to be one of "accept me the way I am" and if it turns out we have interests in common, great, we can spend time together pursuing those interests, and maybe we will become close friends.

For example, if two USAers were talking about favorite movies and one liked the latest action/adventure flicks and the other found such Hollywood offerings totally boring, preferring instead indie films or low-budget psychological dramas, chances are these two would not be seeing many movies together and are unlikely to become friends.

Individualism-collectivism and friendship

Looking beyond cross-cultural comparisons with USAers, how do friendships differ more generally between individualist and collectivist cultures? According to the experts, people in collectivist cultures make greater distinctions between friends and non-friends, than do those in individualist cultures. People in collectivist cultures ignore and can be downright unfriendly toward anyone who is not a friend or family member. They concentrate their friendships on a very small number of people, with whom they are very close and very interdependent, and these relationships tend to be very stable, perhaps lasting a lifetime.

The crucial differences which distinguish human societies and human beings are not biological. They are cultural.

-Ruth Benedict

And, of course, just the opposite is assumed to be the case for people from more individualist cultures. They tend to have larger number of friends with whom they feel less close or interdependent and they don't distinguish much between friends and non-friends, projecting a friendly demeanor to most everyone in their environments. Their friendships are less stable, showing a higher degree of fluidity, with some friendships fading while new ones are just developing.

These assertions about the nature of close friendships in individualist and collectivist cultures were, and still remain, quite pervasive. Nearly all of the major theorists affirm the same conclusions: That individualists cultivate a larger number of more superficial friendships while collectivists tend to focus on a small number of very close and enduring friendships.

Getting started

The most interesting thing to me was the discovery that no one had actually tested these assertions directly and empirically. That is, up to the point when I began my research, no one had ever gone about systematically asking people from a variety of cultures how many close friends they had, how long they had been friends, or taking measures of friendship closeness. They simply used lots of other data about social behaviors in individualist and collectivist cultures from those grand studies described above and inferred they applied to friendship as well.

I tried to address this omission directly beginning in the early 1990s. I conducted a variety of studies in a range of cultures and among international students studying in the U.S., with the goal of comparing USAer friendships with those of other cultures. My results never fully matched up with those assertions. In many cases, I found just the opposite, that USAers reported a smaller number of friends and that they felt closer to their friends than do people from other cultures.

Of course, the story of friendship and culture is a great deal more complicated than just how many close friends people can name, how long they have been friends, and how close they feel toward them. *Friends Beyond Borders* is my attempt to untangle some of these complexities.

Research is the process of going up alleys to see if they are blind.

–Marston Bates

For the reader who is already well versed in the fields of cross-cultural research, what I have done is to take the individualism-collectivism dimension and try to tease out three identifiable sub-dimensions, each producing a pair of opposing friendship styles that compare friendships in the U.S. with those in other cultures. Many of the conclusions derived from this analysis reflect a logical outgrowth of the original individualism-collectivism dimension. But there are also a surprising number of findings that run contrary to expectations.

For those of you with expertise in this field of research, I look forward to your feedback at future conferences. For a complete listing of chapter notes and full references, please visit the website **www.friendsbeyondbordersbook.com**.

Looking ahead

In the next chapter, I'll talk about the first of the six styles of friendship, one I initially found somewhat annoying. In fact, a conference paper I gave about this style of friendship was entitled, "Why is my Asian friend always trying to run my life?"

Chapter 4

Interveners: Friends taking care of each other

I get by with a little help from my friends.

–John Lennon

Take a minute and think about one of your closest friends, someone you care deeply about, someone you see as an important presence in your life.

Imagine the last time you were together. What did you do? What did you talk about? Reflect, for a moment, on why you see this person as one of your best friends.

Now that you have this person firmly in mind, I want you to imagine you are together again tonight, and this time, your friend happens to be driving. You are in the passenger seat. And as much as you love this person, you have to admit your friend is driving a little recklessly and a little too fast. Then the unthinkable happens: In a moment of distraction, your friend hits a pedestrian.

Truth or consequences

You both live through a veritable nightmare of police cars, an ambulance, flashing lights and lots of questions from the authorities. The pedestrian was seriously injured and was taken directly to the hospital. These dramatic events eventually lead to a trial, and as it turns out, you will be called to testify. In fact, you are the only witness to the events of that evening.

As procedures unfold, it becomes increasing clear the outcome of the trial will hinge on your testimony. If you testify your friend was speeding, he or she will most certainly be facing significant time in prison. If you testify your friend was not speeding, he or she will very likely go free. It's all up to you. What would you do?

Before reading on, please decide—will you testify your friend was speeding, or will you testify your friend was not speeding?

Fons Trompenaars, a noted Dutch cross-cultural researcher, posed this scenario to thousands of people in a wide variety of cultures. He found that people differ quite dramatically in what they see as the appropriate thing for a good friend to do. In the U.S., 93% of respondents said they would testify against their close friend, stating he or she was indeed speeding. By comparison, in South Korea, only 37% said they would testify their close friend was speeding. (In the world of cross-cultural research, the size of this difference is extraordinary.)

I've given this scenario several times in my university classes in the U.S., and the discussion invariably turns to issues of justice and fairness, and the consequences of testifying under oath. The typical USAer would feel truly bad testifying against a close friend. Yet, he or she feels no strong obligation to bend the truth just to save a friend from serving jail time, especially since the friend was clearly in the wrong. USAers tend to see it as a matter of legalities, applying the rule of law fairly to all concerned, regardless of personal relationships. Telling the truth is the only fair thing to do in this case.

South Koreans assess the situation quite differently. In their culture, friends feel a strong obligation to protect one another, which leads them to consider that the fair and appropriate thing to do in this case is to stand up for the friend. After all, if you can't count on your friends to stand by you in times of need, whom can you trust? Fairness means being true to one's friends.

Interveners

I call friends who feel a strong obligation and responsibility to take care of each other *Interveners*—they intervene in each other's lives when circumstances call for it. They see it as their duty to advise, aid, protect, take care of, instruct or influence their friends in a positive way.

They often offer assistance even without being asked. Waiting to be asked to provide some service implies one has been insensitive to the needs of a good friend.

On the flip side, *Interveners* expect to be taken care of by their closest friends. They assume that their friends have their best interests in mind and they count on them to do what they think is best to help them out, even if they don't request it. It is what friends do. Based on Trompenaars' findings and other work I'll cite shortly, I argue that *Intervener* friendships are rather common in South Korea.

The Trompenaars' scenario provides just one example of how cultures think quite differently about the expected role of a good friend. He and his team of researchers did several variations on this study, one of which is worth mentioning here. They varied the scenario in terms of the seriousness of the injury to the pedestrian. They found when the pedestrian was more seriously injured, *Intervener* cultures such as the South

> *I'll lean on you and you lean on me and we'll be okay.*
>
> –Dave Matthews Band

Koreans were even more likely to testify in favor of the friend. As a Korean, the motivation boils down to "the more my friend is in danger, the stronger I feel an obligation to protect him or her."

In the U.S., by contrast, people are even less likely to testify in favor of the friend. The more serious the injury, the more the USAer friend feels obligated that justice be served, even though their close friend will have to pay the consequences. Clearly, scenarios like this one serve to demonstrate in very stark terms how very differently USAers and Koreans think about what it means to be a close friend.

In a land of *Interveners*

I got to experience the *Intervener* style of friendship first-hand during my yearlong stay and my subsequent visits to South Korea. Initially, these experiences were a bit unsettling. Having friends who felt it was their duty to be responsible for me was not something that came naturally to my ego, my notions of autonomy and self-sufficiency. I often wanted to say to them, "I can take care of myself, thank you!"

On one particular trip, I was staying with a couple I didn't know well before my arrival. But over the month I stayed with them, we spent hours every evening in stimulating conversations, covering everything from our life histories to the challenges they faced as both parents and professionals. The three of us developed a very intense rapport, and our interactions quickly resembled those of close friends in Korea.

Occasionally, we would go out to eat or take in some cultural event in busy downtown Seoul. On these occasions, we would invariably find ourselves walking along noisy, congested, multilane streets in the busiest parts of the city. To me, the streets in Seoul always seemed hopelessly chaotic.

Whenever it came time to cross one of these busy intersections, the husband of this couple would go into grade-school-traffic-cop mode, dashing out in front, waving his arms to guarantee that cars would indeed stop, to ensure my safety. There were always throngs of us crossing the street at the same time, so actual danger to me was minimal. I initially thought he was clowning around, but in fact, he was quite serious, exercising his duty as a good friend, looking out for my welfare.

I do not wish to treat friendships daintily, but with the roughest courage. When they are real, they are not glass threads or frost-work, but the solidest thing we know.

-Ralph Waldo Emerson

It all felt a bit paternalistic, often controlling, as if my friends were trying to run my life, like I didn't have enough sense to take care of myself. When it comes to giving instruction or advice, *Interveners* can be rather direct and demanding, a characteristic they share with the *Realists* I'll describe in Chapter Nine. As *Interveners*, they are simply trying to help out.

Once I was in the process of sautéing vegetables as my contribution to an international dinner the three of us had attended together. At one point, the wife of this couple directly and forcefully grabbed the utensils from my hands to show me how to do it correctly. On another occasion, I shared with this couple a manuscript I was working on for a journal article about friendships in Korea. I wanted their feedback. They were quite insistent I make significant changes—their advice was uninhibited and adamant, going well beyond what would be the norm in the U.S.

This couple clearly cared about me, even though we had known each other for less than a month. They were concerned for my welfare, they wanted me to succeed, whether that involved crossing a street safely, sautéing vegetables or writing for a research journal.

Spending as much time as I had with Koreans, I long ago grew to interpret these active interventions in my life as warm and friendly, the way they were intended. To me, their actions exemplify the way *Interveners* think and feel about close friends. If a USAer friend had tried to help me cross a busy intersection, taken over my vegetable sautéing or offered such blunt advice for my professional work, I would have seen it as insensitive, intrusive, or at least, unusual.

Cultural stereotyping: A word of warning

I need to pause and take time out here to offer some important caveats. Making such sweeping statements about Koreans must be seen as a generality and nothing more. If you meet a Korean at work tomorrow, don't automatically expect him or her to show *Intervener* tendencies should you eventually become friends.

In fact, we should never assume these global cultural stereotypes apply to any particular individual, no matter how much data support their existence at a national level. I have a very close USAer friend who is a relentless and unreserved *Intervener* and I am sure there are many individuals in Korea who can't relate to my ideas about *Interveners* as close friends. The point is we often don't fit our cultural stereotypes, and it is important we keep that fact in mind whenever I make such sweeping generalizations.

Please excuse me for donning my professorial robes, but I feel a strong obligation to lecture a bit more about the limitations of cultural stereotypes, this time using USAers as an example.

If you are a USAer and have traveled at all, you are probably aware we carry more than just our baggage when we go abroad. We also tote a very pervasive stereotype. Nearly everyone watches our movies and our TV shows, listens to our music, eats at MacDonald's and in other ways consumes our cultural effluence. All of this leaves them with a clear picture of who they think we are as USAers.

I met a lot of people in Europe. I even encountered myself.

–James Baldwin

When the locals see us walking down any sidewalk in Barcelona, Moscow, or Tokyo, they can often identify us as USAers even when they see us at a distance, long before they hear us utter a word. They can reliably pick us out of throngs of tourists. They have us pegged, at least at the superficial level of appearances, and probably much beyond that.

Over the twenty years I regularly taught cross-cultural psychology, I typically spent a lot of class time trying to get students, especially my USAer students, to appreciate the cultural stereotypes others hold about them. At the end of these sessions, I would ask how many of them feel like their national stereotype fit them as individuals. In all those years of teaching this course, no one has ever raised a hand to that question!

So we must be careful in how we think about cultural stereotypes, especially when I make assertions about a particular version of friendship being common to a given culture. It is best to think of these differing versions as friendship "styles" rather than as culturally fixed norms. *Interveners* are but the first of six styles of friendship I'll be discussing, and it is important to appreciate that any of these styles can be found in any culture of the world. We can each cultivate the style of friendship that suits us best, regardless of our culture of origin.

All of these caveats won't prevent me from talking about mainstream norms that dominate or characterize friendships in a specific culture. I do think particular friendship styles are more common in some cultures compared to others. But we must hold these stereotypes with a healthy degree of disrespect. Around the edges of these norms are a myriad of combinations and variations.

In addition, regardless of one's preferred style of friendship, each one of us has probably been an *Intervener* with a close friend at some point in our lives. Friendship styles are much more fluid than fixed; we naturally tend to do what is called for in any given situation. Perhaps you have a close friend who was grieving the loss of a loved one, and you stepped in to take over some critical responsibilities for the friend. In that case, you were being an *Intervener*. It is my hope we can all relate with varying degrees to all six styles of friendship.

Ok, I'll hang my professorial robes back in the closet, and spare you any more lectures.

Intervener or a busy body

The *Intervener* style of friendship came out quite clearly in one of my own studies, which compared the friendship styles of university students in five different cultures. I asked students in France, Spain, the

U.S., Cuba and China to read the following vignette in their own language (and with names common to their respective cultures):

Megan and Cheryl attend the same university and are the best of friends. While they often have fun together and care a lot about each other, schoolwork is one area where they differ. Megan is less interested in school and is only an average student, while Cheryl does well in nearly every course she takes. Cheryl tries to influence Megan to be a better student so she will be successful in life. Sometimes, Cheryl reads over Megan's class notes, making corrections and adding specific information for her to study. Cheryl often insists Megan study when she doesn't really feel like it. Cheryl thinks Megan is too interested in having fun and not sufficiently serious about her work. They are best friends but they clearly have different ideas about school.

They were then asked to rate elements of the vignette along a number of dimensions. Students in France and the U.S. tended to see the friendship as an unhealthy relationship. They saw Cheryl as too controlling—many thought she needed to mind her own business and not try to change Megan to be someone she is not. Cheryl, they argued, must learn to accept Megan the way she is.

Students in China, Spain and Cuba were more likely to see it as a warm, healthy and caring relationship. Cheryl genuinely cared about Megan and was doing all she could to help her out. The Cuban students, in particular, saw it as typical behavior between two good friends.

Whoever says Friendship is easy has obviously never had a true friend!

–Bronwyn Polson

To me, these results imply that the Cubans, the Spanish, and the Chinese students in my sample were more comfortable with the *Intervener* style of friendship. The students in these cultures were accustomed to the idea that good friends naturally take care of each other, intervening in each other's lives, helping them to become better people. To them, these are normal friend behaviors. It is what good friends do.

As an aside, it is interesting to note in this study, unlike many studies of friendship, there were no significant gender differences in the response patterns. Men and women in every culture seemed to have similar perceptions of the nature of the friendship between Cheryl and

Megan. I will discuss gender similarities and differences in close friendships in much greater detail in Chapter Twelve.

Lean on me and I'll lean on you

It is important to note *Interveners* depend on each other and they don't see this dependency as a negative thing, something to be ashamed of, whether this dependency is an aspect of close friendship or a family relationship. *Interveners* see such dependencies as normal and healthy in any close relationship. Even middle-aged adults feel some psychological dependency on their parents.

In fact, it is generally considered unhealthy to be psychologically independent of family and friends. Others would see you as aloof, insensitive, uncaring or cold. For *Interveners*, such dependencies, involvements, and interventions are a critical aspect of feeling close to a friend. It is evidence we are good friends.

Feeling responsible to take care of one's friends gets expressed quite differently among *Interveners* in different cultures. In South Korea, the word *choeng* came up in nearly every discussion and interview I conducted to explain how they felt about their closest friends. *Choeng* is a complex concept, which has received a great deal of attention in the psychological literature devoted to the study of interpersonal relationships in South Korea.

Choeng is typically translated into English as "love" or "affection," fitting terms since it refers to a strong emotional bond and is used most often when referring to family or marital ties. But it carries implications beyond love and affection, including notions of being unconditional, involving sacrifice, empathy, caring, and sincerity. It also implies a common fate—the two friends (or lovers or family members) are destined to be together.

Not in psychological vocabulary

I did the bulk of my work in South Korea between 1994-1996, and as part of this research I made a very surprising discovery, which provides a very telling commentary on the mindset of relationship researchers in the U.S. at the time. I searched the term "caring" in the *Psychological Abstracts* devoted to friendship, and to my astonishment, there wasn't one friendship article using this word as a key search term. Granted, this was before digital search engines became the standard tools of behavioral researchers, but I found it astounding and very revealing that the term "caring" was not in the western psychological vocabulary dedicated to friendship! This is especially surprising given the frequency with which we use the term "caring" as a way of describing someone's character or personality.

In fairness to the sensibilities of professionals engaged in relationship research, there were other terms which came close to the notion of caring, the main one being the expression "social support." Apparently, one can offer "social support" for a friend in the Western version of friendship, but one typically does not take "care" of the friend. Even today, the term "caring" is rarely offered as a search term for studies focused on friendship in the U.S. It is not seen as a relevant aspect of close friendships among Western relationship researchers.

Intervening or intruding?

Korean *Interveners* often express caring for their friends by actively involving themselves in their lives, to an extent that would seem intrusive to a typical USAer. I am not the first to make this point about close relationships in Korea. For example, Jae-Ho Cha in a book entitled *Individualism and Collectivism* (edited by Uichol Kim and others) argued that notions of individual freedoms and rights don't apply to close friendships in Korea, where friends routinely intrude on each other's lives in the name of caring.

I don't need a friend who changes when I change and who nods when I nod; my shadow does that much better.

–Plutarch

In an *Intervener* culture, the interventions of a friend, like Cheryl correcting Megan's class notes, are signs of a close friendship. This style of friendship works best when the receiver of these interventions perceives them as warm and caring, rather than invasive or meddling. As you might have guessed, things don't always work out that way, even in cultures that lean toward the *Intervener* style of friendship.

Such interventions are not always enthusiastically appreciated.

Once at a conference of intercultural practitioners where I was presenting this research, during the question and answer period, a member of the audience raised her hand and exclaimed, "I'm from an *Intervener* culture, and I know all about these interventions from friends, and trust me, they don't feel all warm and fuzzy as you suggest—they are downright annoying!"

I would argue she was probably not oriented toward the *Intervener* style of friendship, but she was stuck living in a predominantly *Intervener* world! Usually, but certainly not always, our friends hold similar assumptions about what it means to be a good friend. If you would find it disrespectful or annoying when a friend aids or advises you, chances are slim you will be cultivating *Interveners* as close friends, which may be challenging if that is mostly what you find around you.

Dealing with unappreciated interventions

The woman at the conference who expressed her annoyance with *Intervening* friends was making the point that unwelcome or inappropriate interventions can stress a friendship. This notion showed up more than just occasionally in my interviews with Koreans. Some would report feeling burdened by taking care of their friends while others would seem annoyed that their friends were trying to run their lives.

People drain me, even the closest of friends, and I find loneliness to be the best state in the union to live in.

-Margaret Cho

Like Cheryl in the vignette study described above, I've heard many a Korean student lament all of the efforts he or she was expending on trying to help a friend make it through his or her course work, deal with a romantic problem or a family conflict. They would talk about their friends as if they were a terrific burden in their lives. I've heard these stories from the other direction as well, students feeling bedraggled, trying to live up to the expectations of a demanding friend. Yet, these students would see their friendships as very close and caring.

Occasionally, I saw cases where a friend's attempts to intervene were clearly not appreciated, like the woman who expressed this sentiment during a conference presentation. It is important to understand how the typical *Intervener* would deal with such situations.

Try to imagine yourself in the shoes of an *Intervener*, and your friend is providing you with unappreciated aid or advice. Let's say your friend is trying to push you toward a career move you feel isn't right for you.

You love this person dearly, but you are quite clear, he or she is completely off base on this one. What can you do? As an *Intervener*, you have different options for dealing with it.

You could disagree, even protest the advice, and the two of you could have a frank discussion, and like the *Realists* to be discussed later, even a heated argument about how each of you sees the matter. These too are things *Intervener* friends do in the normal course of their day-to-day relationship. Or you could graciously accept this advice as something to think about, even though, deep down, you feel you know better than your friend what works best for you and your future. Either way, you would realize and appreciate that your friend cares about you and has your best interests in mind. At least, that's the ideal among *Intervener* friends.

As I hope you will see, each style of friendship has its advantages and benefits but also its drawbacks and pitfalls, and the *Intervener* style is no exception. Ideally, both the giver and the receiver of these interventions will see them as positive gestures of a caring friendship.

Regardless, it can be quite challenging for someone not so oriented to have an *Intervener* friend. The U.S. embodies a very mixed culture with a wide variety of friendship styles, especially in very diverse urban settings. But generally speaking, most USAers are not accustomed to the *Intervener* approach to close friendship and tend to be uncomfortable with it, especially when the interventions run contrary to their self-perceptions or personal preferences.

The USAer perspective

> *My best friend is the one who brings out the best in me.*
>
> –Henry Ford

For the USAer, it may seem at times as though their individuality is being disrespected. Even worse, they might feel badgered or even belittled by the actions or comments intended as aid or advice coming from the *Intervener* friend. Hurt feelings, confusion and resentment are common reactions, leaving the *non-intervener* wondering whether or not this is a true friendship. It is typical in the U.S. to refer to such friends pejoratively as "busybodies" or "control freaks," those who feel it is their responsibility to tell their closest friends what they should do and how they should do it.

On the other hand, *Interveners* can be terrifically loyal and tremendously helpful friends. Their actions reflect their genuine belief about what is best for their friends, and they will expend enormous efforts to help a friend in ways that often prove beneficial in the longer term. When these friendships function at their ideal best, the *Intervener* friend will go well beyond the call of duty to help out a friend in need, in concrete and substantive ways, that would be very uncommon in other styles of friendships. It is my hope you will see the benefits of each style of friendship.

Friends in constant need

Another point worth making about *Interveners* is that the giving and the receiving between close friends can sometimes become lopsided. I have listened to many stories where one friend is doing most of the giving while the other is persistently on the receiving end, and this one-sided state of affairs can go on indefinitely.

Interveners:

*Feel it is their duty, responsibility to take care of their friends

*Advise, aid, instruct, and influence their friends in positive ways

*See dependence on friends as a good, healthy thing

*Often help a friend without being asked

*Can offer critical advice in the spirit of wanting to help the friend

*React to unwanted interventions with rebuttal or silent acceptance

*Can go quite far in their attempts to help a friend in need

*Tend to be unbothered by lopsided giving/receiving exchanges

*Like to do things for their friends

What is interesting is these imbalances rarely endanger an *Intervener* friendship. This inequality may produce some tension and discomfort, yet this lopsided state of affairs, generally speaking, won't cause the friendship to fall apart. The typical *Intervener* seems to have boundless patience for a friend who just can't seem to get his or her act together and is in constant need of support.

In fact, some interviewees have implied, rather than seeing it as a burden, they tend to feel closer to a friend they have helped out over a period of time. When asked to explain, one interviewee said, "My friend is very grateful for all I have done for her. I know we will always be close." In another interview, a Colombian student studying in the U.S. said he had loaned a friend a large sum of money and was in no hurry to get it back. When asked to explain, he said, "I know I can count on his loyalty as a friend."

French *Interveners*?

Interveners are typically from collectivist cultures, and so most of my examples stem from the time I spent in Korea and from interviews I've conducted with people from other collectivist cultures. France, like the U.S., is a very individualist country. Using Geert Hofstede's rankings of 53 countries and regions on the individualism-collectivism dimension, only nine countries score as more individualist than France. (The U.S. is number one on Hofstede's individualist scale.)

So generally speaking, it would not be accurate to refer to France as an *Intervener* culture. My vignette study described above and my survey data would confirm that assertion. However, in my personal experiences, I have found the French to be much more of an *Intervener* culture compared to the U.S. They may not be as blatantly intervening as the Koreans I have known, but I have observed on many occasions that French people tend to do things for their friends.

> If a friend is in trouble, don't annoy him by asking if there is anything you can do. Think up something appropriate and do it.
>
> –Edgar Watson Howe

Raymonde Carroll, an anthropologist, has written insightfully on this point in her charming book entitled *Cultural Misunderstandings: The French-American Experience*. In providing assistance to friends, she argues, the French are more likely to volunteer help without being asked, whereas in the U.S., friends typically wait to be asked for help. (This is a common feature of *Intervener* friendships anywhere—helping out a friend without being explicitly asked to do so.)

In the U.S., to take the initiative to help out in some way without being directly asked, in other words to actively intervene, would imply that the receiver of the aid is incompetent or overly dependent. And these are rather taboo sentiments in this individualist-minded culture.

What follows is a personal anecdote exemplifying the French tendency to be more *Intervener* than we USAers. It concerns a couple I have known since the early days of my sabbatical year in Paris. I consider the husband to be among my closest friends. Whenever I come to Paris, I always rent an apartment, an inexpensive way to stay for a couple of weeks and benefit from non-touristy locations. On one of my trips, my regular rental agent called me at the last minute, informing me there had been a mix up and I wouldn't be able to stay in their rental for this trip as I had done many times in the past.

No problem, said my friend, who insisted I stay with them, something I had been avoiding since I worried they would feel overly obligated to "host" my visit. We had a long phone call discussing the matter, and I insisted they go to no special bother on my account. I would bring a sleeping bag, and camp out on their sitting room floor. I knew their home well and I made the point repeatedly that I would be quite fine with my sleeping bag. They agreed.

Well, I arrived to discover this couple had completely vacated their bedroom, including removing most of their clothes from the armoire! For my stay, they had moved into a tiny shed at the end of their back yard. I was flabbergasted! Of course, I, with my USAer mentality, felt very ill at ease with this arrangement, realizing the extent to which I had put my friends out—in this case, putting them out literally. It is no exaggeration to say I felt ashamed and embarrassed.

I've told this story a number of times. When my listeners are USAers, they seem understandably astonished that my hosts would literally move out of their house in order to accommodate me. They assume I am either bragging about what good friends I have, or this couple suffers from some psychological insecurities that they should go to such great lengths to host me. When the listeners are French, many (but not all) can't understand why I was embarrassed. More typically, they comment I must have good friends who care about me. But they also mention such a gesture would not be out of range of a consideration they might show to a good friend.

Friendship is always a sweet responsibility.

-Kahlil Gibran

For that memorable trip to Paris, while I was surprised and taken aback by my friends' kindness and generosity, I tried (and hope I succeeded) in reacting appropriately—deeply touched and grateful! I did my best to be a gracious guest to my very gracious hosts. I view their kind gesture as an example of the kind of thing an *Intervener* would do for a friend.

Interveners, not always collectivist

Intervener leanings may also be found in other individualist cultures. Reactions I have received from presentations at conferences for groups of interculturalists lead me to think that some northern European cultures, which are typically rated as highly individualist, might also have a tendency to be *Interveners* in their friendships. While I have not conducted research in any of these countries, it is my contention that the prevalence of *Intervener* style friendships in a culture is only weakly related to the dimension of individualism-collectivism discussed in Chapter Three.

An additional point here is *Interveners* not only "intervene" in the lives of their friends, they are simply more likely to do things for them. I could write dozens of such stories. I think closeness for *Interveners* is, in part, reflected in the extent to which friends actually do things for each other. They may be tiny things, they may be symbolic in some way that is significant to the friendship, but they carry a weighty message, that I care about you, that I enjoy pleasing you, that you are important to me.

Looking ahead

USAers would express such sentiments quite differently. As *Independents*, they respect each other's autonomy, and any help offered a good friend would take a very different form.

Chapter 5

Independents: Respecting a friend's autonomy

It is not so much our friends' help that helps us as the confident knowledge that they will help us.

–Epicurus

"Frankly, Americans don't know how to be friends!" I heard this statement and many like it from international students in confidential interviews I conducted over the years I worked at Winthrop University. While this rather severe assessment wasn't the dominant sentiment of most internationals, I heard it often enough to leave a lasting, poignant impression. Research by Elisabeth Gareis, a communications researcher who has also focused on cultural differences in close friendships, has repeatedly shown that international students are often frustrated in their attempts to make friends with USAers.

After I had adopted friendship as my new line of research, I would ask for volunteers from among the international students studying at Winthrop each semester to allow me to interview them confidentially about their friendship experiences. I was especially interested in their friendships with the USAer students they encountered in their classes every day. I would meet with these students individually at the very beginning of their stays at Winthrop, and then periodically throughout each semester.

Even after just a few semesters, a rather clear and consistent pattern developed in their friendship stories. At the very beginning of their sojourns, these students would invariably be very excited about their new adventure of living in the U.S., and they were enamored with the openness and friendliness of the USAer students they met. They were certain they would soon have rich friendship stories to share with me in the near future. These initial interviews were always so positive and optimistic.

In subsequent interviews, I mostly heard about their disappointments and confusion. I should note there were exceptions to this pattern, students who developed very close and satisfying friendships with their USAer cohorts, but most students found themselves frustrated in their attempts to develop such close friendships.

The friendships which last are those wherein each friend respects the other's dignity to the point of not really wanting anything from him.

–Cyril Connolly

I tried to make it a habit to interview my volunteers one additional time in their final weeks on campus, at the end of their studies, just before they returned to their home cultures for good. I would ask them about their experiences at Winthrop, about their friendships, and whether or not there were other students they were planning to stay in contact with after returning home. More than half would say they hadn't made a single USAer friend, that their closest friends, the ones they planned on staying in contact with after returning home were other international students studying at Winthrop.

Their experiences recalled those assertions I had read earlier by Alexis de Tocqueville, written more than a century and a half ago, that USAers are an open and friendly people, but that close, abiding friendships are rare among them. As I mentioned in Chapter Three, the idea that USAers don't cultivate close friendships is astonishingly pervasive in the cross-cultural literature. In manuals written for study-abroad students, whether they are aimed at students coming to the U.S. or USAer students about to go abroad, they all say the same thing: USAers are not oriented toward making close friendships. Similar statements can be found in cross-cultural textbooks written by psychologists, experts in communications or other disciplines. Even in the international business literature, everyone seems to agree: We USAers don't make great friends.

A very different story

Over the years, I also surveyed thousands of USAers of all ages and personally interviewed hundreds of them, and it has always amazed me that USAers' depictions of their own friendships rarely approximate the negative international reputation others in the world hold for them. The vast majority of them, both men and women, claim to have very good and satisfying friendships. They would say things like, "My friends have gotten me through some very tough times," or "I have friends who mean the world to me."

> *Let us be grateful to people who make us happy; they are the charming gardeners who make our souls blossom.*
>
> –Marcel Proust

When total strangers in the U.S. learn I do research on close friendship, many will launch into these incredible stories about a friend they've had since childhood. It is so clear from their stories, these friendships really do mean the world to them. While not all of their reports are so dramatic, the vast majority of them claim their friends hold a very important place in their lives.

There have been exceptions, of course. A surprising number of middle-aged men, for example, would say they didn't have even one person in their lives they thought of as a close friend. But the vast majority of people I surveyed and interviewed would relate these heart-warming stories about the importance of friends in their lives.

Facing the paradox

For years, I was baffled by the contradiction between what USAers were telling me about their close friendships and what the cross-cultural literature and international students would tell me about USAers and their disinterest in close friendship. At times, I began to wonder if there wasn't a built-in bias in my surveys and interviews: Perhaps only those USAers who had close and satisfying friendships were willing to participate in my research projects. I think there is an element of truth in this conjecture. Yet I varied my sampling methods and survey strategies, and these touching, positive appraisals would continue to flow in unabated.

I eventually came to the conclusion there is another way to think about these issues. Perhaps USAers do cultivate close and satisfying friendships, but they simply differ from other cultures in how they think about and behave toward their closest friends. These cultural differences are so profound, so ingrained, we seldom give them a passing thought. Only those who have made a major cultural shift at some point in their lives, whether this was the result of immigrating to a new culture, or spending extended periods of time abroad as a student or an expat employee, only these people might be aware of the fact that their friendships in the new cultures had a very different feel to them compared to those back home.

Even world travelers may not develop an awareness of the cultural differences in close friendships. Lots of people who spend extended periods in a new culture tend to confine their social lives to others from their home culture, thus depriving themselves of these fresh experiences.

But for those who do make the effort, whole new worlds of friendship await them. These open-minded individuals may develop some awareness of the fact that friendships in one culture can differ quite dramatically from those of another. And for those coming to the U.S., initially at least, they don't recognize the USAer version of friendship as the real thing.

Independents versus *Interveners*

So what is the USAer version of friendship? I call it the *Independent* style of friendship. As the word implies, *Independents* tend to respect each other's autonomy and freedom. *Independents* can have very close and satisfying friendships, but unlike the *Interveners* of the last chapter, they wouldn't think of meddling in each other's lives unless they are invited to do so or unless they are certain such interventions would be welcome. To do otherwise would be disrespecting a friend's individuality, violating their self-respect.

Independence is happiness.

–Susan B. Anthony

They feel no strong obligation to take care of their friends. Each individual is responsible for him or herself.

A close *Independent* friend

A friend is one before whom I may think aloud.

–Ralph Waldo Emerson

So if they don't feel a need to take care of each other, if they don't intervene in each other's lives, what exactly does it mean to be close, *Independent* friends?

The nature of these friendships came out most clearly in the interviews I conducted in the U.S., where this style of friendship tends to be very common. While I tried to always maintain a strictly scientific approach to my survey research, my interviews tended to be more freewheeling and open-ended. I could spend hours listening to people's friendship stories.

When USAers were telling their stories, I would be surprised at how often they would say things like, "I've had some tough times—I wouldn't have made it without my close friends." Such expressions were common in the stories of both the men and women I interviewed. I always asked for an explanation, "How have your friends helped you through rough times?"

They would typically tell me about some very difficult period in their lives, something to do with a health crisis, or a troubling problem at work, or perhaps a major upset in their romantic lives, "and my friend helped me through the entire ordeal!"

"What exactly was it your friend did to help you through the entire ordeal?" I would persist. "Well," they would say, "my friend came to visit me in the hospital," or "We spent hours on the telephone every night during that entire period," or "He took me out to get totally smashed and put up with me crying in my beer all night long!"

The most basic and powerful way to connect to another person is to listen. Just listen.

–Rachel Naomi Remen

The fact is *Independent* friends tend to help each other out simply by being present, by being good listeners and sounding boards, by words of encouragement to boost the morale of their friend who has a problem. And these are very powerful supports in the world of *Independent* friends! The listener may offer to help out in some concrete fashion, and that offer might be accepted, but often it is not.

The friend relating the problem eventually comes away from the conversation feeling better about the issue at hand, realizing he or she has a close and caring friend. He or she will feel like the friend really helped out in dealing with the problem, when in fact the friend may have been little more than just a sensitive and supportive listener.

Independents feel genuinely supported when they know their good friends are aware of their current challenges and are wishing them well. They feel they have a friend who stands by them through thick or thin.

The power of fun

While these kinds of stories came out quite frequently in my interviews with USAers, and served to explain what it means to be a close friend in the *Independent* version of friendship, most of their time spent with close friends had little to do with a health crisis or a major disappointment in their romantic lives. Mostly, they just spend time with friends having fun.

And having fun is important. It is easy to underestimate the consequences of this aspect of close friendships. *Independent* friends simply value and enjoy each other's company. They love spending time together, doing things, engaging in conversation, laughing, and appreciating the break away from the busy work-a-day world. These are critical elements in their definition of what it means to be a close friend.

Happiness never decreases by being shared.

–Buddha

USAers, at least when compared to most western Europeans, have longer workweeks and many fewer vacation days. Their work tends to be highly competitive, their employment insecure, and the supports for those who lose their work are comparatively sparse. In a word, their work lives are highly stressful.

So time spent with friends, getting away from work, having fun, engaging in some mutually enjoyable activity or simply having coffee, drinks or a meal together, are highly valued among *Independent* friends. This may seem like a shallow and meaningless version of friendship to some, but these are precious moments for *Independent* friends. And as we will see in Chapter Eleven, these precious moments can have a powerful influence on friends' overall wellbeing in addition to buffering them against minor and major stresses in life.

The shifting sands of friendship

It is true that USAers, especially those who cultivate the *Independent* style of friendship, tend not to depend on each other in ways that would be commonplace among *Interveners*. Jan Yager, a sociologist, has written a fascinating book entitled *Friendshifts*, a term she coined to illustrate the "modern approach to friendship" where people swap out old friends for new ones as they go through life's many changes, such as taking on a new job, moving to a new address, getting married or divorced, or even earning an advanced degree.

Viewing her ideas from a cross-cultural perspective, the book seems squarely aimed at USAers. She warns the reader against depending on one's friends and emphasizes the importance of having fun, keeping things upbeat and positive, all qualities I see as defining what it means to be an *Independent* friend.

An *Independent* way of life

Being independent-minded isn't just a style of friendship for USAers, it is also, in many respects, a lifestyle. USAers value independence as a personality characteristic. In the U.S., we raise our children to be independent from a very early age, allowing them to make basic decisions for themselves like what clothes they will wear or what they want for breakfast. This tends to be true of other individualist cultures as well.

Kids are encouraged to have their own opinions and, at least among middle class USAer parents, to speak up and express themselves in family discussions. We try to maintain this sense of independence throughout our lives—even the frail elderly stubbornly resist any semblances of dependence on the family, since any kind of dependence is seen as an unhealthy negative.

USAer ideas about independence are evident even in the connotations of the term. When I first attempted to learn the Korean language, I was fascinated to discover that the words "dependent" and "independent" have almost opposite implications and feelings in English compared to Korean. Apparently, this applies when comparing English to many other languages as well. In English, the word "independent" carries mostly positive connotations. It is good to be independent minded, to have an independent attitude, and we admire people with an independent spirit.

Independents:

*Encourage and respect their friend's individuality, autonomy

*Value spending time together, lowering stress, having fun

*Are good listeners, sounding boards, for friends with problems

*Offer encouragement to boost friend's morale during difficult times

*Prefer maintaining a strong sense of independence in their friendships

*See their independent spirit as adaptive and healthy

*Tend to keep score when giving/receiving aid to ensure equality

*Value "being there" for friends, but don't see this as a duty

The word "dependent" carries mostly negative associations in English, implying someone is weak, vulnerable, helpless, needy or addicted to something that is not good for them. USAers like to think they can take care of themselves; they don't need other people intervening in their lives. Even psychologists in the U.S. consider any sort of dependency as unhealthy for one's psychological wellbeing.

Long lists of best-selling self-help books are aimed at helping people lose their unhealthy dependencies on alcohol or drugs, on unhealthy relationships, or on compulsive eating habits. Some have even suggested it is unhealthy to become dependent on rigorous daily exercise!

In the Korean language, as is true apparently of other Asian languages as well, the connotations of "independent" and "dependent" are just the opposite. They see being dependent as a very positive thing, especially being dependent on one's family, which is highly valued throughout one's life.

There is a current trend among young Asian parents to raise their kids to be more individualist and thus more independent minded, but it will probably be some time before the connotation of these words change. The negative implications of the term are so strong that, in some contexts, calling one "independent" can be downright insulting. As I mentioned in the last chapter, it can imply one is aloof, cold and uncaring.

Accept me the way I am

Independent friends do respect each other's autonomy, and in that sense, their relationships appear, at least to others, to be more distant or unfeeling. USAer friends, who often represent the *Independent* style, do not intervene in each other's lives, since that would feel invasive, smothering or disrespectful. They don't typically tell each other what to do or how to live.

The conventional maxim seems to be: If we are to be friends, you must accept me the way I am and not try to change me. Trying to influence me to change implies you don't really like me.

The lack of any obvious sense of dependency, the fact that they don't actively intervene in each other's lives, the emphasis on just having fun with friends, the tendency to build up their friends' egos with words of encouragement, all of these characteristics leave USAer friendships appearing shallow and uncommitted to many people who come from abroad. As I've mentioned, nearly all cross-cultural social researchers hold this view of USAer friendships. In addition to my work, there are other studies that call this picture into question. I would like to delve into some of that research.

Whose friendships are closer?

When relationship researchers actually measure and compare relationship closeness across cultures, the results are seldom clear-cut. In fact, quite often cultures that prefer the *Independent* style as their preferred version of friendship, like the U.S., score higher than do *Intervener* ones on a variety of measures of relationship closeness. There are reasons to suspect the validity of such measures when applied across cultures, but nevertheless, there is very little empirical evidence to suggest that USAers do not cultivate close and satisfying friendships.

> *Friendship improves happiness and abates misery, by the doubling of our joy and the dividing of our grief.*
>
> –Marcus Tullius Cicero

A fundamental problem in much of the cross-cultural research aimed at these issues is the fact that it conflates "closeness" among friends with being "dependent" on them. It is not difficult to imagine situations where one resents feeling dependent on others, even close friends. In my interviews with *Interveners*, the negative side of these dependencies would surface from time to time, and from both perspectives, feeling burdened by an overly needy friend and resenting having to depend on a friend for some aspect of one's day-to-day life.

Further complicating this issue is how we think about "depending" on a friend. Let's say that whenever you get in a jam, you have a friend who steps in to take care of your children while you are busy dealing with the problem. Or your friend offers you her car when yours is in the shop. In these cases, being dependent means you and your friends actively "intervene" in each other's lives, by doing things for each other when situations call for it. The assumption among most cross-cultural theorists is that friends who take care of each other, depending on each other in these concrete ways, would have to be very "close."

But there is another way of thinking about the issue of dependency between friends that is more in line with the *Independent* style. I could depend on my friend for having fun, for example. My life is stressful and having someone to play ball with or meet over coffee helps me keep my sanity. And when I am going through a particularly bad time, my friend provides a respite from life's hassles, which I find revitalizing, and motivates me to deal with life's issues more productively. This is a very valid version of closeness and interdependency, even though less overt or concrete.

For it is in giving that we receive.

–St. Francis of Assisi

My point here is closeness in friendship is not equivalent to dependency. USAers can be good friends without feeling a responsibility to actively take care of each other.

In describing close friends, sociologist and author Jan Yager got it right in asserting, "whether or not you do lean on your friends during a crisis, you should feel that, *if* you wanted to, you *could*." In my interviews with USAers, they often reported that feeling, although they rarely had concrete examples of friends actively intervening in their lives.

What *Independents* do

This is not to say *Independent* friends never do things for each other. They help out when explicitly requested or when they are certain the offered assistance will be appreciated. Even so, *Independents* will normally limit such interventions to insure that the receiver doesn't get the message that they are incompetent to handle their own affairs.

Research also points out that the *Independent* who receives such aid will try to reciprocate the favor in some fashion as soon as possible and thereby reduce the discomfort they feel about "owing" the friend. When it comes to doing things for friends and friends doing things for us, *Independents* prefer keeping score. They keep track of these exchanges with the explicit goal of making sure the accounting sheet stays in balance. I will invite my long-time friend out to dinner as compensation for him mowing my lawn while I was out of town.

To keep friendship in proper order, the balance of good offices must be preserved, otherwise a disquieting and anxious feeling creeps in, and destroys mutual comfort.

–Charlotte Bronte

To be clear, some score keeping is characteristic of all friendships, regardless of friendship style or culture, especially newly developing ones. If two people are slowly becoming friends, it is common for them to monitor their investments in the relationship as a way of determining if the interest is mutual. One typically stops making gestures of friendship if the other doesn't reciprocate. This pattern occurs in new friendships anywhere in the world. But once a close friendship is established, *Independents* will continue this line of thinking much more than *Interveners*.

A sense of duty is useful in work, but offensive in personal relations. People wish to be liked, not be endured with patient resignation.

–Bertrand Russell

Independents keep score as a way of preserving their own sense of autonomy in the relationship. They may do things for each other from time to time, but they don't want to feel dependent, and keeping score helps them sustain a sense of equality with their friends. And when *Independent* friends do things for each other, these gestures aren't the kinds of unsolicited interventions common among *Interveners*. When *Interveners* do things for their friends, by contrast, there is also a much stronger sense of obligation or duty than is common among *Independents*.

Independents rarely think of friendships as involving duties. They don't feel responsible for their friends. Friends are supposed to "be there" for each other, to help out with understanding and encouraging words, but these expectations are not thought of as duties or responsibilities.

Duties and privileges

In his recent book on friendship entitled *Friend v. Friend* Ethan Leib argues quite persuasively that the privileges as well as the duties of close friendships should be enshrined in our laws and public policies in the U.S. Such laws already exist for married couples, he notes, why not for close friends?

For example, in a criminal case, spouses are not required to testify against each other. Close friends should have the same privilege, he argues. Similarly, one should be entitled to work leave for taking care of an ill friend the way spouses often do.

In terms of duties, he argues, if a close friend sells you her house, she should be held to a higher standard for disclosing potential problems with the house or the transaction. In legalese, this is referred to as a fiduciary relationship, akin to that between a doctor and patient, or between a lawyer and client, and implies a level of trust that would extend beyond that normally assumed between the home seller and buyer.

Similarly, an agreement with a friend would be binding, even if it weren't put in writing. Again, he points out, the law should recognize the special, trusting relationship between friends, both in terms of privileges but also in terms of duties. He goes into great detail about other such duties of friendship, such as privacy and reasonable protection from harm. He qualifies all of his assertions in significant ways such that his arguments end up being unexpectedly cogent and convincing. Leave it to us USAers to turn the duties of friendship into the basis for litigation!

A friendship story

To render all of these ideas a bit more tangible, I will offer a hypothetical case study demonstrating what might happen when an *Intervener* and an *Independent* try to forge a mutually satisfying friendship between them. This story is based loosely on a composite of actual events I witnessed while living in South Korea.

In this story, George is a USAer preferring the *Independent* style of friendship, while Dae-Jung is a Korean who tends toward the *Intervener* style.

George is 32, a new arrival in Seoul working as the local representative of an advertising agency contracted by a Korean automaker to develop an ad campaign for the U.S. and other international markets. Dae-Jung is 33 and a professor of English at a major university in Seoul. George is seeking a tennis partner to continue his passion for the sport in his new environment and he is introduced to Dae-Jung through work associates. Even after just one match, the two realize they have similar levels of both skill and desire to practice the sport as often as possible.

Dae-Jung helps George obtain a membership in his racquet club, no small feat given the connections required for gaining admittance. They play often, typically two or three times a week, and they usually spend ten or fifteen minutes chatting afterwards while sitting on benches to cool down. Most of their talk revolves around tennis, about critical plays in the matches they just completed as well as watching and commenting on the play of others.

They also begin talking about other things. Dae-Jung is married with a three-year-old boy. He has spent time in the U.S. and Australia as part of his education and also for vacations. George is single, having broken up with a woman just prior to being assigned to Korea. He enjoys living in Korea and is viewing it as an opportunity for a fresh start. He is working hard to learn the language and to accommodate to the local foods and customs. Each man has a sense of humor and they are quick to find ways to poke fun at each other's game. George is constantly telling jokes that aren't always fully appreciated by Dae-Jung, who assumes something is getting lost in translation.

Around the third week, Dae-Jung invites George out with him and his family for dinner at a Kalbi restaurant to enjoy some local barbeque. They meet at the restaurant, and George discovers that Dae-Jung's wife has brought a friend along, and as the evening unfolds, it becomes evident the couple was trying to introduce him to a potential woman friend. He finds the woman attractive, but communications are awkward since she speaks little English and he is just beginning to learn Korean. He wishes Dae-Jung had warned him in advance of his matchmaking intentions, rather than leaving him to sort through the confusing signals he is getting from both the woman and the couple. The whole evening is a bit uncomfortable and embarrassing.

Both men laugh about it at their next tennis outing—Dae-Jung jokingly trying to figure out if the match between George and the woman has potential to develop into a budding, intercultural romance, and George making fun of Dae-Jung's attempts at playing Cupid. In fact, George is not interested in any serious dating at this point, with everything so new and unclear compared to the dating scene at home.

At about this same time, Dae-Jung discovers George is still living in a hotel because of the difficulties in obtaining a furnished apartment. George's assignment in Korea will probably not extend beyond two years and finding appropriate lodging compatible with that time frame is not easy.

Dae-Jung has a cousin who owns an apartment that is available and could be furnished to meet George's needs. They agree to check it out together but George finds it quite small and doesn't like its location, which is at some distance from his work. Dae-Jung is quite insistent he take it, since it is unlikely George can find a better deal. George feels Dae-Jung is being much too pushy, and eventually has to insist he isn't interested in renting the apartment, regardless of what a good deal it will be.

At one point, Dae-Jung complains about the difficulty he has in securing internships in local industries for his students studying English. George, with all of his connections in the advertising and auto industries, offers to see what he can do. But nothing ever comes of it.

Story analysis

Let's look back over this case and analyze it from the perspective of the two styles of friendship we have discussed so far. The experiences of George and Dae-Jung exemplify the potential for conflicts when an *Independent* and an *Intervener* try to forge a mutually satisfying friendship. Both enjoy playing tennis and their post-game chats, but Dae-Jung is constantly frustrated by George's unresponsiveness as a friend. Dae-Jung helps him gain membership in the tennis club, introduces him to an attractive woman and in other ways tries to intervene in his life as a friend should.

The world only goes round by misunderstanding.

–Charles Baudelaire

When George complains about his living arrangements, Dae-Jung even finds him an apartment, yet George seems clearly unappreciative. George doesn't seem to raise a finger to help him find internships for his English students.

From George's perspective, he enjoys the companionship of Dae-Jung, but also feels at times manipulated, or that Dae-Jung is being too pushy, not allowing him to make his own decisions. Dae-Jung is fun and caring, but just a bit too controlling, constantly wanting to take over and run his life. It is hard to get him to take "no" for an answer.

For Dae-Jung and George to develop a mutually satisfying friendship, they will have to compromise on their *Intervener* and *Independent* notions about what it means to be a good friend.

It is worth noting that the misunderstandings occurring between Dae-Jung and George could easily occur within any given culture, including between friends in the U.S. In this case, however, we would be more inclined to think of the differences as reflecting their individual personalities rather than their cultural backgrounds. Dae-Jung might be seen as generous and perhaps a bit too controlling, George as fun, but maybe somewhat insensitive. For this reason, it is best to think about *Interveners* and *Independents* as two opposing styles of friendship, rather than fixed, culturally determined entities.

Looking ahead

Interveners and *Independents* not only hold very different ideas about what it means to be a good friend, they also communicate in very distinct ways that would also put a friendship between the two at great risk, which is the topic of the next chapter.

Chapter 6

The spoken and the unspoken

The language of friendship is not words but meanings.

-Henry David Thoreau

I felt so bad! I had assured my new Korean friend on several occasions I would purchase the alcoholic beverages he needed for his father's big birthday bash. The family patriarch would be turning 60 and it was to be a very big affair, traditionally one of the grandest days in a person's life in Korean culture.

My teaching position on military bases in South Korea included PX privileges, which allowed me to purchase scotch, bourbon, vodka and gin for about half of what it would cost on the open market. However, I had recently learned that purchasing alcoholic beverages for Korean nationals was illegal and I didn't want to break the laws.

The lady doth protest too much, methinks.

-Shakespeare's Hamlet

I felt really bad about disappointing my friend. As I apologized, he seemed truly put off, looking to the side, sighing, trying to talk about something else, but I wouldn't let up. I continued to explain my situation, especially the risk of losing my position. The more I talked, the more he grew impatient with me.

Eventually I figured out that apologies don't typically work the same among friends in Korea compared to the U.S. In retrospect, I think my friend did accept my apology and appreciated how badly I felt. The problem was I explained too much.

Words and more

This chapter is about the differing ways *Interveners* and *Independents* talk with their close friends, and the ways each apologizes for a wrongdoing is a prime example of this difference. *Interveners*, and I clearly see this friend in that category, don't see the point of long, detailed apologies. Such apologies are largely seen as unnecessary among close friends. They seem to think "love means never having to say you're sorry," the iconic line from the Eric Segal novel and 1970 film, *Love Story*.

Communication scholars such as Edward T. Hall have devoted a great deal of research to the communication patterns of *Intervener* or collectivist cultures compared to *Independent* or individualist cultures, and this chapter is based largely on their work. Stated most simply, *Interveners* put less stock in words as a form of communication.

People communicate in various ways, and from an *Intervener's* point of view, words are greatly overrated. Koreans and others Hall refers to as "high context" cultures pay more attention to what is imbedded in the relationship of the communicators. Two *Interveners* in conversation would consider each other's background, status or role in society and the immediate context where the conversation is taking place.

What you do speaks so loud that I cannot hear what you say.

-Ralph Waldo Emerson

If one person is a teacher and the other a student, each person's role, age and status speak volumes. A few words from the teacher might cover all that needs to be said. For *Interveners*, much is already understood, simply from the context. Spelling things out in words would leave both sides uncomfortable—it just feels unnecessary.

Independents have just the opposite approach, emphasizing words, using them very explicitly to convey information, feelings and wishes. USAers, especially those who espouse the *Independent* style of friendship, believe any human exchange should be based on good communications, and by this they mean verbal communications.

A teacher talking with a student would spell things out in great detail, providing a rationale for whatever is being discussed, and the student might even make statements or ask questions to clarify that rationale. Hall refers to this as the "low context" style of communication, where the context is largely ignored and words are the primary vehicle by which individuals convey their thoughts.

The difference between the two styles of communication can be subtle, but the implications are far reaching. I'll provide examples of both styles to show how they play out in everyday life and then return later to their impact on close friendships. Both styles can be effective and nuanced in communicating information, wishes and feelings. The key difference is that the *Independent* style depends almost entirely on words, whereas the *Intervener* style makes full use of a variety of channels of communication.

Intervener movies

The *Intervener* style of communications is evident in the movies of countries like Japan or Korea. As *Intervener* cultures with less emphasis on verbal communication, there is less dialogue and therefore fewer subtitles to read, no small advantage to those of us who read slowly. But *Independent* minded USAers often experience a different frustration. In these films, tensions often build around some misunderstanding between the main characters, and USAers can't understand why the protagonists don't just sit down and have a good, long heart-to-heart talk to straighten things out.

A typical theme in Asian romantic movies, for example, is unrequited or frustrated love. Let's say that in one such film, a serious misunderstanding arises between two people who have just fallen in love. A common reaction among USAers is to think, why doesn't she just tell him, why doesn't she simply explain that the man he saw her with was a cousin, and not a rival admirer? If she just explained it all, he would understand and everything would work out fine for them. But in *Intervener* cultures, it is not the norm to spell everything out in words.

Words are cheap

In fact, spelling things out this way would generally not feel reassuring for *Interveners*, and this would apply in any kind of close relationship. For *Interveners*, intimate or supportive talk of any sort, especially long verbal exchanges, do not typically promote warm and caring feelings in the same way they would for *Independents*.

For example, if you were going through tough times in your life due to the death of a loved one or a serious problem at work, a good friend's words of comfort would be less comforting if you espouse an *Intervener* perspective on your close friendships. By contrast, a kind or thoughtful deed might communicate at a much more profound level.

Even romantic relationships depend less on intimate talk in *Intervener* cultures. I had read that in Korea, men rarely say things like "I love you" to their wives. I asked a Korean gentleman who was about my age whether this was true. This was someone I had met on a couple of occasions, and from all appearances, seemed quite devoted to his wife and three daughters. So I was taken aback by his response to my question.

> *The most important thing in communication is to hear what isn't being said.*
>
> –Peter F. Drucker

"Oh definitely it is true," he said, shaking his head and looking very serious. "If our relationship was in such bad condition that I had to tell her I loved her, well," he paused for quite a long time, continuing very deliberately, "it would mean our marriage was in very bad shape and I was desperate to save it."

The lesson here is that for *Interveners* words can cheapen deep sentiments. His love should be obvious from his actions, the way he treats her, the trust they've built over the years. To express these feelings in words would somehow defile the sacredness of this trust. *Interveners* value what is not said, what is implied or inferred. Understanding what someone is saying without putting it into words is considered more precious.

I should add, however, this idea that words can demean romantic feelings might be waning, at least in today's younger generations. I know of a young Korean couple who regularly express their affections by leaving Post-it notes for each other in the bathroom, on the refrigerator, on the television, etc., saying simply, "I love you."

The power of words

For *Independents*, words carry the entire message, especially for sharing deeply held feelings. Other channels of communication often go unnoticed, as if they didn't exist. This is most evident when a person's verbal message contradicts other channels of communication, such as facial expressions, gestures or tone of voice. For *Independents* what the person is saying will dominate the message the listener takes in.

Laura and Brenda, for example, have been best friends since college and one aspect of their friendship involves playing tennis every Saturday. They meet for lunch one day, and Laura asks Brenda if they could skip tennis this Saturday because she met a new guy at work and they talked about going to a local flea market together at that time.

Brenda is miffed. The two of them have always considered their tennis outings as sacred. Brenda works hard and their matches are about the only vigorous exercise she gets all week. She tells Laura she really wants to play and isn't there something else she can do with her new friend? Laura says this would be her first time with the guy away from work and she didn't want to pass it up.

Eventually, throwing up her hands in defeat, Brenda relents, and with disappointment in her voice, a scowl on her face, she says, "Okay, okay, go to the flea market with your new guy!"

Now, will Laura attend to the verbal permission she was given, or the obvious discontent Brenda expressed nonverbally? While this example may be a bit exaggerated, *Independent* USAers tend to put more weight on the words rather than the conflicting non-verbal cues. Often these cues go completely unnoticed. Only the words matter.

Tuning in

Intervener-minded Koreans would be much more attentive to non-verbal cues in any exchange. They tune into each other at

The human body is the best picture of the human soul.

–Ludwig Wittgenstein

a very physical level. How we sit or stand, how we hold ourselves says a lot about our character and maturity. They notice and take into account our tone of voice, facial expressions and eye contact. All of these non-verbal channels are speaking quite loudly. They may be saying volumes about us, often communicating messages we are only dimly aware of, such as our hidden attitudes about the topic of conversation.

These non-verbal cues are especially communicative of our emotions, our current mood, and how we feel about what is being discussed.

During my stays in South Korea, I often ask for advice from USAers I happen to meet who enjoy living in this culture. These would be individuals who speak the language fluently, have adapted well to the norms and customs, and seem to be thriving in their adopted culture. I like to ask them what particular things newcomers should know about Korean culture that would help them get along better. Most respond with comments about showing interest and respect for their culture, and learning about their history. But one USAer businessman's response stands out from all the rest, and I will quote his exact words, which were delivered with sincerity and passion:

To know another's language and not his culture is a very good way to make a fluent fool of yourself.

–Winston Brembeck

"The thing most Americans fail to appreciate about Koreans is that every conversation, every exchange, whether it be at the highest or most formal level, or simple day-to-day exchanges about mundane matters, all exchanges begin, are sustained and end on an emotional plane. Once you learn to tune into this emotional dimension of each and every interaction, you will have more productive and satisfying relationships with Koreans."

Essentially, this USAer gentleman was trying to teach me how to communicate sensitively and effectively in an *Intervener* culture. It is still a difficult lesson for me to absorb, as an academic who has made his living in the world of words.

Interpreting only the words

While I was teaching there, one of my students was a Korean woman who was married to a USAer military chaplain. She was truly bi-cultural, with nearly perfect English, having lived in the U.S. for extended periods of time. After she completed my course, we would meet for lunch from time to time, since I loved getting her perspective on so many questions I had about Korean culture.

Because of her linguistic skills, she often served as an interpreter between USAer and Korean military officers. At one of our lunch get-togethers, she arrived a bit late and visibly agitated. She was upset about a meeting she had just attended where she was interpreting between USAer and Korean base commanders. Their dialogue concerned a controversial decision the USAer general had made, and she was intensely frustrated that her role was to only interpret the words and not what was actually being communicated.

According to her, the communications of one were completely bypassing those of the other. In fact, she fumed, they weren't communicating at all!

The Korean wasn't asking the USAer to rescind his decision. But that's all the USAer "heard," repeating his decision, saying it was final, that there's no room to compromise. Restating his response only served to exacerbate tensions. From the Korean commander's point of view, the decision was producing difficult ramifications, and he simply wanted the USAer to understand his predicament.

Silences make the real conversations between friends. Not the saying but the never needing to say is what counts.

–Margaret Lee Runbeck

My student argued the outcome of the exchange could have been much more positive and productive had the USAer commander fully appreciated and responded to the implied messages of his Korean counterpart.

How's your *kibun*?

The *Intervener* style of communicating plays out differently in each culture, but they have in common a tendency to deemphasize verbal forms of communication. I am focusing on South Korea because my experiences living there provide a rich source of examples. Before bringing the focus back to friendship per se, I'd like to explore other Korean norms concerning their tendency to communicate in ways other than words.

Kibun is an aspect of Korean culture that plays an important role in any social exchange. It is a dimension of communication Koreans automatically attend to. A USAer military contractor I know well said his Korean wife asked him every morning how his *kibun* was doing. *Kibun* is typically translated into English as "mood," but that's a very lame equivalent. It is a bit like asking, "How are you doing today?" with implications that run far deeper. *Kibun* covers a wide range of issues, like, "Are you in a good mood?" "Are you happy?" "Are you optimistic about the day?"

It also hints at how you feel physically, "Are you comfortable in your own skin?" In this same conversation, the military contractor said, only half jokingly, "*Kibun* includes whether or not you had a satisfying bowel movement that day!" Koreans tune into each other's *kibun*, and their perception of your *kibun* will influence how they react to you. If you have bad *kibun*, chances are they will know it and treat you accordingly, such as avoiding you or approaching you with caution.

I think we USAers are blithely walking around with our *kibun* hanging out for the entire Asian world to see, without our least awareness of this mode of communication.

Silence can be golden

Cultures with an *Intervener* style of communication such as South Korea also tend to be more comfortable with silences in the course of any conversation. In the U.S., such silences are usually interpreted negatively, as pouting, disagreement, or a lack of social skills. If you and I are conversing, and you suddenly remain silent, I would naturally think something's wrong, that you are upset about something I said, that you are willfully ignoring me, or that you are distracted by something you see as a higher priority than our conversation. In any of these cases, my perception of your silence is negative.

Deafness has left me acutely aware of both the duplicity that language is capable of and the many expressions the body cannot hide.

–Terry Galloway

I should note that Koreans could view such silences negatively as well. But more often, silences can relay positive information, especially about one's feelings. Silence can be quite communicative. Here is a personal example.

During my first yearlong stay in South Korea, I made only two close friends. Frankly, having two *Intervener* Korean friends was nearly a full-time job! A great deal of my free time was spent with the friend I was hopelessly apologizing to at the beginning of this chapter. I often had the pleasure of having dinners, going on outings and attending local events with him, his wife and his extended family.

However, one aspect of these occasions was always a bit awkward—how to conduct myself with his father. As the oldest male, and the patriarch of the family, everyone showed him deference and respect. As a guest, I too was given a position of honor. Where we sat at table, who was in the lead car on family outings, all such circumstances were complicated and left me uncertain about what to do. I was perfectly willing to live with lower status, but that wasn't for me to decide.

One warm spring afternoon, we were all together hiking up a steep trail in a national park, on our way to enjoy a family picnic. The father was leading the pack, some twenty feet ahead of the rest of us. I saw this as an opportunity. I sped up and walked next to him, actually at his side but just slightly behind him. We walked together like this, away from the rest of the family, for some time. I didn't say anything and he didn't either. We simply walked together until we reached the grounds for the picnic.

Even though not a word was spoken, there was a strongly felt connection, because of our physical proximity, our mutual enjoyment of nature, walking together and sharing each other's company. I was certain he felt this connection as well.

Drawing on my fine command of the English language, I said nothing.

–Robert Benchley

Evidence for this new rapport between my friend's father and me came a little later when we were all seated on the ground, legs crossed as is customary, enjoying all the wonderful food that had been prepared for the occasion. He was sitting right next to me, and at one point, he leaned completely across my legs, practically lying on my lap, while reaching for a bowl of kim-chee. It was obvious the two of us had reached a new level of mutual comfort. And all of this was accomplished without a word of explanation, no apologies for my past awkwardness, no expressions of affection. Silence can be a powerful communicator!

Silence as a form of communication, the concept of *kibun*, non-verbal cues, the role of emotions and contextual factors like one's status or position, all of these are examples of the *Intervener* tendency to focus on elements in their social exchanges in addition to the words being spoken. Among *Interveners*, there is little felt need to fully explain how one thinks or feels. They are more attuned to what is not said, what is implied or already well understood by both parties.

Getting back to friendship

Independents and *Interveners* often have a hard time adjusting to each other's style of communication, and I'll turn to those issues next, which will serve to bring the discussion back to close friendships.

First, their differing communication styles can easily generate mistrust in both directions. The excessive wordiness of *Independents* sounds like they are trying to cover something up, make excuses, or belie their true feelings. The lack of explanations on the part of *Interveners* seems like they are hiding something, not telling the whole truth. These opposing styles can undermine friendships between *Interveners* and *Independents*.

Secondly, silences in the course of conversation can be difficult for *Independents*. I'll use myself as an example. Despite my story above describing my "communicative silence" with my friend's father, I more typically felt awkward with silences in my conversations with Koreans, especially with my psychiatrist friend, who was quite instrumental in helping me conduct my friendship research in South Korea.

Talking is like playing on the harp; there is as much in laying the hands on the strings to stop their vibration as in twanging them to bring out their music.

–Oliver Wendell Holmes

As part of this undertaking, we got together frequently, and after each meeting, I often felt I had done nearly all of the talking. I tried steadfastly to rein in this tendency, but never came close to mastering it. Any pause at all in our conversations and I would fill it with words, lots of words, usually explaining something or other that was probably already obvious, just to keep the conversational ball rolling.

Quite frankly, the silences made me uncomfortable, even though in reality, they may have lasted only a few seconds. And when she did speak, I felt so relieved to hear what she had to say I would anxiously jump over her words with still more of my own. Obviously, I wasn't a very well-attuned listener!

Many of our conversations revolved around friendship research, and I was rather obsessed with methodology, data collection and interpreting the results, while she viewed my work with a wider lens, commenting on its implications for understanding Korean culture. In many of our regular meetings, I didn't quite appreciate what she was telling me until after the fact. Usually her comments would take a day or two to sink in, when I would finally arrive at a sort of eureka moment, like a flash of insight, leaving me with a deeper appreciation of what she was trying to tell me.

We always spoke in English. Unlike my French, my Korean never got to the point of being conversationally functional, despite my best efforts. But she had an excellent command of English and always seemed to choose her words carefully, sometimes stating things indirectly, rather than directly and explicitly. As I will clarify later Koreans can be quite direct and forceful in their communications with close friends. However, in this case, she often explained things in a fashion that required time on my part to decipher the true meaning.

Communicating friendship

The area where these two styles have their greatest impact within close friendships concerns how we communicate closeness to a good friend. For the *Independent*, this process depends very heavily on talk, particular kinds of talk.

When I would ask my USAer psychology classes what it means to have a good friend, one of the first responses was nearly always the feeling of being able to talk about anything, even very personal matters, and know the friend would still accept them. Sharing personal information promotes mutual acceptance and trust. Good *Independent* friends know a lot about each other, based largely on talk about personal likes, dislikes, past experiences, feelings, personal successes and failures. These exchanges are seen as privileged information, the kind of thing one would only share with a close friend.

The time has come, the Walrus said,

To talk of many things:

Of shoes and ships and sealing-wax

Of cabbages and kings

And why the sea is boiling hot

And whether pigs have wings.

–Lewis Carroll

Western social psychologists have studied this self-disclosing talk for decades. It's considered a key indicator of closeness in USAer friendships. Women usually score higher compared to men on these measures, but the principle applies to all *Independents*. Self-disclosure is the primary means of developing a sense of closeness in their friendships, especially during the early stages of a new friendship.

Interveners and talk

The friendships of *Interveners* depend much less on this type of talk. To be clear, good friends talk, and such talk is the essential commerce of all close friendships the world over, regardless of style of friendship. In my survey studies, nearly all agreed that they could tell their closest friends things they wouldn't share with anyone else. The key factor is the kind of talk and the role it plays in cementing their friendship.

Self-disclosing talk plays a much more minor role in friendships between *Interveners*. I saw this fact play out many times among the international students trying to befriend more *Independent*-minded USAers. *Intervener*-minded international students were surprised and often puzzled by how quickly the USAers would talk about personal matters, their preferences, their past experiences, even potentially embarrassing things like their fears or failures. It often left them uncomfortable, not knowing how to respond, especially when the revelations were embarrassing.

Sometimes the international students would interpret such disclosures as the USAer being modest or self-effacing. But they would quickly discard this idea since it was clear the USAer was seeking social approval—they wanted the international student to somehow indicate they still liked them, despite the personal faults or problems that were just revealed.

At a year-opening social event at my university, I once overheard a USAer student mention in a conversation with a new international student that he had been taking Ritalin since early childhood. The international was initially dumbfounded, not knowing how to respond to this personal revelation. He then said rather meekly that those drugs have long-term consequences and he hoped the USAer student was no longer taking them, advice that could be seen as a normal *Intervener* reaction.

In situations like this, an *Intervener's* natural tendency is to step in and do something or, in this case, give rather direct advice on how the USAer should think about the issue. But *Independent* USAers aren't seeking and don't welcome such corrective reactions. They would feel rejected or at least disrespected. The USAer would see it as an unfriendly thing to say.

From the *Independent's* perspective, the lack of constant, clear and self-disclosing talk from the *Intervener* is seen as disinterest in friendship, suggesting a barrier to open, heartfelt communication where they share each other's likes, dislikes, experiences, even personal fears or weaknesses. It is difficult for the *Independent* USAer to feel close to a person who keeps so much of his or her identity a "secret."

Other paths to friendship

But again, it would be incorrect to conclude that talk is unimportant for *Intervener* friends—it is simply less important, especially the self-disclosing version of friendship talk. Among *Interveners*, rather than place so much importance on talk, a key factor in feeling close to a friend could be simply the passage of time. A developing friendship requires years to mature, repeatedly spending time together, nourishing a repertoire of shared enjoyable memories.

Some of these times together may not have been so enjoyable, as in cases where friends have survived some of life's challenges together. Basic training in the military or the trials of pledging a fraternity can lead to some lasting friendships. Having this common history allows each to know the other well, one's strengths and weaknesses, and how each reacts to a wide variety of circumstances. This intimate knowledge is gained not through self-revelations, but through lived and shared experiences. These times together form the foundation of trust and companionship, allowing each to feel like they have a close friend. Among many *Interveners*, there is no easy substitute for time—there are no short cuts to developing a close friendship.

In addition to spending time together and developing a repertoire of shared experiences, another factor indicating closeness among *Interveners* can be a history of mutual interventions in each other's lives. *Interveners* tend to do things for each other, to help each other out, but also as a way of communicating closeness and caring.

These interventions work a bit like self-disclosure does among *Independents*. They tend to start out small, dealing with superficial or inconsequential issues. But for a friendship to develop these interventions must be mutual, they must be reciprocated, and over time, they become more personal and sensitive to the needs of the other.

If someone beats me handily at my favorite sport, handball, and then proceeds to give me advice on how to improve my game, I could see this behavior as arrogant and annoying. Or I could accept the advice, taking it as a gesture of goodwill and friendship. If I should similarly intervene in my handball opponent's life, it could be the beginning of a new friendship, leading to a series of mutual commitments cementing our relationship.

Up to this point, I have been using Koreans as examples of *Intervener*-style communicators. However, cross-cultural research suggests that self-disclosure doesn't play the critical role among friends in many cultures of the world as it does for USAers. From my experience and research conducted by others, the French are clearly less comfortable self-disclosing with close friends compared to USAers. Some have argued that we in the U.S. are rather extreme in our tendency to disclose personal information.

Interveners and apologies

I would like to go back to the story I used to open this chapter, since apologies make for such blatant examples of the difference between the *Intervener* and *Independent* styles of communication. Recall that I was stubbornly trying to apologize to my Korean friend for breaking my promise to provide him and his family with discounted alcoholic beverages for his father's 60th birthday party.

Apologizing - a very desperate habit - one that is rarely cured. Apology is only egotism wrong side out.

–Oliver Wendell Holmes

When it comes to apologies, like all forms of communication, *Interveners* deemphasize words, assuming that if the relationship is strong and trusting, if the friends have a secure sense of confidence in each other, then a long, detailed apology shouldn't be necessary. From an *Intervener* perspective, such explanations begin to sound insincere, show a lack of trust, or as mere attempts to justify one's thoughtlessness.

My friend's reactions to my insistent apologies were telling me to just shut up and let it drop, but I wasn't "listening." He likely appreciated how badly I felt, so why talk about it, why spend the time dwelling on this unfortunate situation since there was nothing to be done about it anyway.

In its place

If *Interveners* don't apologize, then what do they do instead? How do they try to make amends? What is the *Intervener* equivalent to an apology? *Interveners* may apologize as a way to repair any potential damage to the relationship, but such an apology would be brief, lacking details or explanations. Or, in the case of a close friendship, they may do or say nothing at all, preferring instead to let the incident pass, without drawing undue attention to it. They might see it as proof of a deep and unshakable trust. Some might even see the lack of an apology as a test of that trust.

A stiff apology is a second insult... The injured party does not want to be compensated because he has been wronged; he wants to be healed because he has been hurt.

–G.K. Chesterton

But if the *Intervener* still feels a need to make amends, instead of apologizing, he or she could do or say things that would put the broken promise in the larger framework of a caring friendship. The *Intervener* could draw on his or her knowledge of the friend, their long history together, to somehow find a way to bolster or celebrate their friendship. He or she could bring up some cherished event from the past, a camping trip or a birthday party, changing the mood, laughing together as they recollect these fond memories.

Holding true to their *Intervener* style, they could also do something for the friend, offering a special gift or favor, to express how important the friendship is to them. This is not a tit-for-tat compensation, like the scorekeeping more characteristic of *Independent* friends, but rather, a generalized attempt to ensure that the friendship is on good terms, that no harm was done by the broken promise. One way or another, the *Intervener* will manage to foster good feelings and promote the relationship in an affirming way, overshadowing any hurt feelings caused by the broken promise.

Interveners know how to make amends without talking explicitly about the troubling issue.

Let's talk it over

For *Independents*, the way to deal with any kind of relationship difficulty is to talk about it, openly and honestly, often in great detail, perhaps even repetitiously so, making sure each understands the other. Mutual understanding and acceptance grow out of these heart-to-heart discussions, washing away any resentment or hurt feelings.

Intervener Talk	*Independent* Talk
Minimal apologies for broken promises	Detailed apologies for broken promises
Less word-oriented communications	Very word-oriented communications
Words can cheapen deep sentiments	Words can express deep sentiments
Attend to non-verbal cues	Mostly ignore non-verbal cues
Kibun as communicative	No equivalent to *Kibun*
Social silences as positive or negative	Social silences as nearly always negative
See wordiness as insincere or a cover-up	See wordiness as an attempt at clarity
Talk as less central to friendship	Talk as central to feeling close to a friend
Less comfortable with self-disclosure	Self-disclosure as key to feeling close
Closeness depends on time, shared experiences, mutual interventions	Closeness depends on self-disclosure, knowing and respecting each other

Stories

These differing styles of dealing with conflict can cause confusion and tension in the friendships between *Interveners* and *Independents*. This issue comes up often in my conversations with USAers about their friendships with *Interveners*, even USAers who have traveled a great deal and lived in other cultures for periods of time.

Their stories typically involve scenarios where a conflict arose between them, and the *Intervener* just wanted to let it go and move on without talking about it or working through the problem. The *Independent* USAer often ends up with hurt feelings, especially when he or she feels wronged and expects an apology or at least an explanation.

I've heard so many versions of this story! And then, the *Independent* USAer is totally baffled when the *Intervener* continues to behave as though they are still good friends, often changing the topic, making light of the situation. For the *Intervener*, the friendship was never in question. By avoiding any long explanations or apologies, the *Intervener* thought he or she was sparing the friendship any harm, rather than causing it.

As you can see, both *Independents* and *Interveners* desire to amend the relationship after a difficult conflict, but they each employ quite different strategies to reach that goal. I hope these explanations about our different ways of communicating leave you with a variety of ways to think about such situations in your own friendships.

Looking ahead

Have you ever spent time in a culture where people are downright unfriendly? They don't smile, seem to ignore you completely, leave you feeling unwelcome, maybe even invisible. It's easy to think these are sour people who lead bitter lives, and see no value in friendship at all. These appearances can be very deceiving. The next chapter explores the *Excluder* style of friendship, where their outward unfriendliness conceals warm hearts and generous spirits for those they hold most dear.

Chapter 7

Excluders: Are you with me or against me?

A friend to all is a friend to none.

–Aristotle

Whenever I have the pleasure of spending time in Paris visiting my friends, I always marvel at the transformation they undergo on those occasions where they must interact with people they don't know. This could be a waiter in a café, someone seeking directions out on the street, or a neighbor they don't know well. Whenever these situations arise, their personalities seem to go through a marked Jekyll-and-Hyde metamorphosis to the point where I almost don't recognize them as the same warm, loveable human beings I know and love. It doesn't happen every time, but often enough to be striking.

I could cite numerous examples, but I'll tell a story dating back to my first year in Paris, only because at that point, I was unaccustomed to this way of behaving, and found it rather shocking. It concerns a friend I'll call Jean-Paul, and although he and I have drifted apart over the years, we were quite close that year and saw each other about once a week.

To create a sense of this person, I should explain that one of our favorite topics of conversation was classic French literature. We could become quite nerdy talking about Balzac! He was a warm, affable, bookish sort of guy who earned his living as an accountant by day, but by night, he enriched his life with more literary pursuits.

Jean-Paul's entire demeanor would change whenever he interacted with strangers. His facial expressions would go from openness and warmth to outright rigidity and coldness. His tone of voice became deeper, more assertive and authoritarian. Like most French people I know, he was always polite, but it was a clipped sort of politeness that seemed to say, "I don't want to talk to you any more than I have to."

I like Frenchmen very much, because even when they insult you they do it so nicely.

–Josephine Baker

It always struck me as rather hostile, even aggressive, as if he were working up to a good argument.

Milquetoast lets it rip

To set the stage for this story, I ask you to consider the stereotype of the hostile and haughty French waiter, a caricature that is not difficult to validate in many cafes or restaurants in Paris. If you've spent any time there at all, you know what I'm talking about. Jean-Paul and I, along with two others, were having lunch at a restaurant one day, and we were dueling with a particularly acerbic example of this genre. The waiter was impatient, unwilling to answer simple questions, and seemed distracted, causing two of us to have to repeat our orders. Any response we did get from him dripped with condescension.

At one very dramatic point, Jean-Paul had had enough, turned to him and let loose with a tongue lashing that left him with eyes wide open and utterly speechless. He disparaged the waiter's professionalism, made some comparison to a cow, and questioned the man's integrity, all in one snappy little sentence. I had no idea my mild-mannered, cerebral friend was even capable of such insults! I was shocked, although our companions hardly seemed to take notice. And then, almost instantly, he returned to our conversation, where he was his typical, warm, jovial self, as if nothing at all had happened.

Whenever I witness such stark transformations in one of my friends, I want so badly to ask them about it. And occasionally I do. But they nearly always seem reticent to discuss the matter. I get the impression they are mostly unaware of the contrast I see in their demeanor. It all transpires with an ease and naturalness that defies self-awareness.

This kind of thing happens often. I recall a more recent incident with a friend where she was interacting with her next-door neighbor, and the formality and coldness with which she dealt with him left me wondering if there had been some conflict between them. She said no, it was just her neighbor, someone, I learned, she encounters with some regularity.

Defining the terms

These incidents exemplify what I refer to as the *Excluder* approach to friendships and all interpersonal relationships, where clear distinctions are evident in their demeanor and behaviors toward friends, close work colleagues and family members, compared to everyone else. They can go from a relaxed, smiling playfulness with friends to a cold, almost antagonistic approach to everyone else.

According to my taxonomy, the opposite of *Excluders* are the *Includers*, a style more characteristic of USAers, who make no noticeable distinctions in their outward behaviors toward those they know well and those they don't. *Includers* display a generalized friendliness toward everyone— they are just friendly people.

If you have only one smile in you, give it to the people you love. Don't be surly at home, then go out in the street and start grinning good morning at total strangers.

–Maya Angelou

Classic theorists in cross-cultural research, such as Geert Hofstede, Harry Triandis, and Edward T. Hall, have written much about these two social patterns as they apply to family, work colleagues, neighbors, and friends. Much of this chapter is based on their ideas. They hold that the *Excluder* approach is more common in collectivist cultures, although many have noted that the French, who score more toward the individualist end of this continuum, tend to be somewhat *Excluder* in their approach to their social lives.

I should also mention upfront that there is one aspect of my findings that is inconsistent with their work. They hold that *Includers*, like many USAers, have a large number of only superficial friendships while people from *Excluder* cultures tend to have a very small number of much more intimate friendships.

While this may seem to be the case from outward appearances, my findings suggest that USAers do make important distinctions in how they think about their closest friends. On confidential surveys, they will typically identify a very small number of people they see as close friends who play important roles in their lives. I will come back to this issue in greater detail in the next chapter, but for now, suffice it to say, when it comes to the number of close friends, *Excluders* and *Includers* don't seem to differ.

Life as an *Excluder*

In this chapter, I would like to develop a feel for what it is like to espouse an *Excluder* approach to one's interpersonal relationships. *Excluders* see their closest friends as being very different people compared to everyone else, as a very exclusive in-group, not unlike family members. With their friends, they can let down their guard, relax, and just be themselves.

Do other men, for they would do you.

–Charles Dickens

With everyone else, there is a rather natural suspicion or at least a presumed lack of trust—who knows what they might be up to? *Excluders* tend to assume everyone harbors ill intentions until they have proven themselves trustworthy. One must constantly be on the defensive, on guard, with anyone who is not well known.

The French and their attitude problem

USAers visiting France, especially in Paris, often comment about how unwelcoming or unfriendly the French can be. As a Francophile, I seem to be a magnet for ranting commentaries on this topic from USAer acquaintances, which I typically try to make light of. But clearly, many USAers take these reactions personally, concluding that all French people dislike them.

Indeed, there certainly are some French who don't care for USAers, as there are some USAers who don't have a nice thing to say about the French. What I would like to ask you to consider is that the French, generally speaking, are not friendly toward anyone they don't have a personal relationship with, including each other. They are "unfriendly," in the USAer sense of the term, with everyone, which is characteristic of their more *Excluder* orientation.

What does it mean to be friendly?

As I mentioned earlier, since the time of de Tocqueville, cross-cultural researchers and other social commentators have characterized USAers as "open and friendly." But it is worth exploring the idea that what constitutes "friendliness" may itself differ over cultures.

I have worked with many business and civic groups coming to the U.S., and they are nearly always touched by the friendliness of USAers, finding their *Includer* approach to others very attractive and welcoming. However, I suspect that those same "friendly" behaviors might not leave the same impression in many settings around the world. A USAer, wearing a friendly, ear-to-ear grin, approaching a French person on the streets of Paris asking directions can appear a bit goony, immature, and uncultured. The French person might easily perceive it as arrogant and presumptuous, because it assumes a relationship that, from the French perspective, doesn't exist.

As one who has traveled back and forth quite a lot, I've always found it fascinating that the French and USAers each see the other, stereotypically speaking, as a bit arrogant. In part, this perception stems from their different notions of friendliness. The USAers see the French as arrogant for their lack of friendliness and the French see USAers as arrogant because of it. This is but one example of how our differing notions of friendship can have far-reaching consequences.

> Loving people live in a loving world. Hostile people live in a hostile world. Everyone you meet is your mirror.
>
> –Ken S. Keyes, Jr.

The French, of course, can interact easily with people outside their inner circles, but these conversations are marked by the use of elevated, polite language, reflecting the formality expected by such exchanges. Strangers in France who have not been introduced but who, because of circumstances, are required to interact typically do not behave in an overtly friendly manner. For public exchanges at work, in a café, or on the street, people who don't know each other typically won't smile, for example.

Translating friendliness

As most readers probably already know, unlike English, French has different words for "you" when addressing someone formally versus informally. These different levels of language are characteristic of

Excluder cultures. Over time, as people become acquainted, and their relationship grows closer, at some point they make the transition from using the formal to the informal version of "you." For an outsider, when to make this simple transition can be a very thorny affair.

Despite spending a lot of time in France and speaking the language reasonably well, I must confess I don't have a high degree of confidence about when it is appropriate to make this shift to the more informal level of language. Early on, I tended to make the switch quite readily, thinking I was communicating warmth, acceptance and a desire to put the other person at ease.

I saw it as a "friendly" gesture. But like many USAer notions about friendliness, it is easy for this one to go awry. Rushing this transition can come off as clumsy, presumptuous, and even socially aggressive. For *Excluders*, being accepted into the inner circle, even linguistically, can be a delicate matter.

Further complicating this issue, the customs for moving to the informal address are strongly influenced by region, social class, and age (or differences in age) of the people involved. Nowadays, as a rule of thumb, I wait for the French person to initiate the change. As a result, I have one French acquaintance I have known for over four years and we still use the formal level in conversation. Others have moved to the informal with little fanfare early in our acquaintance. It is all still a bit of a mystery to me!

The invisibility of strangers

In Asians cultures, the *Excluder* mentality becomes much more pronounced. In South Korea, for example, they take the distinction between people they know and those they don't to such an extent that members of the latter group don't even register in everyday consciousness. If I were a Korean, people I don't know, with whom I have no relationship, wouldn't actually "exist" for me. It's almost as if they're extras on a film set where the viewers are focused on the main characters and everyone else simply fades into the background.

I'll describe some ways the *Excluder* approach to social relationships plays out in day-to-day life in South Korea before returning the discussion to close friendships.

The streets of Seoul are nearly always quite crowded, and while walking down the sidewalks, it is not unusual to rub shoulders with complete strangers. Occasionally, it can be more than just rubbing shoulders—one gets the impression of being knocked around a bit. It can be truly bothersome for the uninitiated, especially for USAers, who walk around with these enormous invisible protective bubbles, a kind of "no fly" zone where no one but their romantic partners or close family members are allowed admittance.

Perhaps only those people who are capable of real togetherness, have that look of being alone in the world.

-D. H. Lawrence

I live in Charlotte, North Carolina, a very low-density city, and this personal space bubble seems even larger than in the more crowded metropolitan areas of the U.S. At the gym, for example, people I encounter will say, "excuse me" even if they are five feet away and clearly have nothing to be "excused" for. We in the U.S. are accustomed to a lot of personal space, and become quickly uncomfortable when this space is violated.

Koreans are much more accustomed to bumping shoulders with other pedestrians along the busy streets of Seoul. The fascinating thing about these accidental encounters is they almost never result in a polite apology such as "excuse me." For the most part, Koreans, as more extreme *Excluders*, don't even notice either bumping or being bumped by passersby. Everyone else out on the street is so far out of their range of conscious awareness as to simply not "exist."

Most of all, do not hide ... your total indifference to others. Let this emptiness, this profound indifference shine out spontaneously in your smile.

-Jean Baudrillard

Bumper/bumpee observations

I was so taken by this phenomenon I began to watch for incidences whenever I was on a busy street in Seoul. Once I sat in a café in the arts district during lunchtime and watched throngs of people walking by. I found examples of bumping shoulders nearly every minute. Yet, I rarely saw someone acknowledge the other person in the encounter. I watched carefully, and couldn't even detect a sideward glance, no "excuse me," no look of irritation, nothing. Neither the "bumper" nor the "bumpee" seemed remotely aware of the other.

I rarely saw exceptions to this rule. Once, a well-dressed young business man was speaking in an animated fashion with his work colleagues and made a very sweeping gesture with his arms, with the end result of knocking an equally well-dressed young woman nearly to the ground. I assumed he would stop, say something apologetic, and ensure she was okay before continuing on his way.

Nothing of the sort—he simply kept walking. She made the briefest, subtlest expression of frustration with the guy before arranging her clothes and continuing on her way. In my entire year in South Korea, it was one of only a handful of times where I witnessed the "bumpee" acknowledge the existence of the "bumper."

I, the pushy USAer

I'll describe another, more personal and rather intriguing example. Before arriving in South Korea, I had read a great deal about their cultural norms and understood fully the notions of personal space and how Koreans require much less of it in public settings compared to USAers. In time, I became comfortable with this cultural norm and was able to ignore the crowding, bumping, and general press of bodies when out in public.

Still, even months after my arrival, I would at times grow weary of the close contact and frequent bumping I experienced in the subways and buses, on the sidewalks, in theatres, and elsewhere. To help make my way with Koreans, I did learn to speak some of their language, a task I found enormously difficult, despite my best efforts. The Korean language is extremely complex, both linguistically and in terms of the social norms that guide its everyday usage. And my attempts to use it often exposed my social naiveté.

We are all full of weakness and errors; let us mutually pardon each other our follies. It is the first law of nature.

–Voltaire

Once when I was in a movie theatre, seated, waiting for the film to start, three teenage boys needed to get by me, but they came with such speed and force I wasn't able to stand and provide some space for them to pass in front of me.

I felt thoroughly trampled.

As the last one stumbled across my knees, I blurted out "excuse me" in Korean, with a voice that, I'm sure, echoed my frustration. It was a phrase I had never been taught in my Korean language courses, but rather, something I had explicitly searched for in a phrase book, without fully appreciating its social implications.

Well, they all reacted like I was some kind of cruel ogre. They instantly turned to me, bowing deeply, repeating several times their own expressions of apology, and this continued for perhaps 30 seconds or a minute, seeming to me like an eternity of bowing and mumbling.

I described this incident to my friends who explained that what I had done was to suddenly assert my "existence" to these young boys, and now that I had forced myself into their consciousness, and I was much older, they had to show proper deference. It turned into quite a memorable scene, one I never repeated.

These examples give you a taste of what it is like to live in a culture of *Excluders*.

Returning to friendship

Excluders, when not with family, expend most of their social energy and have most of their social needs met by a very small group of intimate friends whom they see often. They are most comfortable and happiest when they are in the company of these close friends.

While these friendships are extremely important to them, it is worth noting and also somewhat paradoxical that *Excluders* don't actively seek social approval from these close friends. Compared to *Includers*, whom you will read about in the next chapter, *Excluders* care a lot less whether or not others like them. They don't seem to need much morale boosting or ego stroking from their close friends. It is not important to them that their friends see them as wonderful human beings. These are not normal *Excluder* ways of thinking about and behaving toward their best friends.

Don't walk in front of me; I may not follow. Don't walk behind me, I may not lead. Just walk beside me and be my friend.

–Albert Camus

Excluders are secure in the knowledge that these close friends will always be there for them—they seem to take it all for granted. The social approval of people they don't know doesn't matter since, as I've just explained, these strangers don't "exist" for them. They don't expect strangers to like them or be friendly toward them. And the same rule applies, to a somewhat lesser degree, to their friends. They seem less hungry for social approval in general, strangers and friends alike.

On the other hand, *Excluders* are concerned about maintaining social harmony and they systematically cultivate positive feelings in their group exchanges. But this is not the same as expecting everyone to like them. Social harmony has more to do with preserving smooth, unruffled relationships with others.

As we will see in the next chapter, *Includers* demonstrate just the opposite tendency. With their open, friendly ways toward close friends and strangers alike, they feel a very strong need to be liked by everyone.

Social skills for closeness

Excluders have a distinctive approach to socializing with their closest friends. They have developed a special set of social skills that make it easier for them to enjoy spending extended periods of time with these friends. Geert Hofstede and Harry Triandis, pioneers in the cross-cultural field, refer to these abilities as "social skills for closeness or intimacy." These skills allow *Excluders* to be at ease in dealing with the closeness that comes with prolonged contact.

I'll use a common example to illustrate this point. Suppose that a small group of friends has decided to spend a two-week vacation together. Already, it is worth noting that this kind of decision is much more characteristic of *Excluders* compared to *Includers*. The latter, generally speaking, would never plan to spend that much time with the same group of friends, thinking, "Yes, they are good friends, but two weeks with them would be just a bit too much!"

Stay is a charming word in a friend's vocabulary.

–Louisa May Alcott

Excluders enjoy this kind of extended "quality time" with close friends. Their well-developed social skills for closeness help them manage the interpersonal frictions and conflicts that naturally arise with prolonged togetherness. Spending two weeks together, they must negotiate everyday decisions such as who is going to prepare the next meal, or where they will go if they are going to eat out, deciding what sites they will visit next, planning the next day's activities, who is driving, who is paying for what, how long they will stay in each locale. Everyday, they will be making a myriad of group decisions.

Excluders, with their social skills for closeness, are quite adept at such negotiations, and they can tolerate, or simply ignore, the interpersonal stresses that living together naturally produces. They are more accepting of each other's idiosyncrasies—thinking, it's okay, it's just the way he or she is. They are skillful at dealing with a wide range of interpersonal issues when it comes to their closest friends.

Conflicts do arise from time to time, and they can become dramatic and long lasting. But in general, they have ways of getting past most difficulties, allowing everyone to save face. Mostly it is just a matter of paying little attention to such social problems, going on with life, enjoying the moment. They are very likely to end their two-week vacation as close friends, a testament to their highly developed social skills for closeness.

Personal examples

As I am writing this, a French friend is planning to visit my wife and me for two weeks in a couple of months. In fact, I've spent long vacation periods with French friends on a number of occasions, and I'm always impressed with how the group dynamics manage to work themselves out. We typically develop a level of comfort and familiarity that never fails to touch me deeply. There is a real sense of family, where both caring and interpersonal frankness seem to coexist in equal measure in our day-to-day interactions.

What counts in a relationship is not how compatible you are but how you deal with incompatibility.

–Leo Tolstoy

Occasionally, when I'm in the midst of one of these experiences, I can't help but wonder how things would be different if my vacation companions were USAers. As I mentioned above, it is unlikely my USAer friends would ever commit to spending such an extended time together, no matter how much we enjoyed each other's company. For the typical USAer, the joy of togetherness lasts for about a weekend, and not much beyond. More than that, I'm certain we would be arranging to spend at least some of that time apart, each doing our own thing, pursuing our individual interests. While I can think of exceptions, in general, we USAers are just not oriented to spending such long periods of time with the same friends.

Of course, my examples here are confounded by the fact that we USAers rarely get more than a couple of weeks' vacation per year, considerably less than anywhere else in the economically developed world. Why is that anyway?

The taboo of social promiscuity

There is one point of conflict that comes up in my relationships with *Excluder* friends that is worth mentioning here. In fact, if I'm not attentive, I don't even see it as a potential source of conflict.

Whenever we are out together and in conversation in a public setting, like a restaurant for example, I'm often much too open to chatting with others around me. My *Excluder* friends tend to see my social promiscuity as off-putting and inappropriate. It is simply not the norm for *Excluders* to be chit-chatty with everyone in sight. In recent years, I've successfully learned to rein in this tendency.

There are plenty of acquaintances in the world; but very few real friends.

–Chinese Proverb

Being openly social is much more common in the U.S., even in large metropolitan areas, such as New York. My wife and I spend several weeks a year in Manhattan and various parts of Brooklyn, and I'm always struck by how often, over the course of a day, we find ourselves having a rather congenial exchange with total strangers, despite New Yorkers' reputation throughout the U.S. of being gruff and unfriendly. These brief, though meaningful, conversations might easily give one the impression we are acquainted, at the very least. These kinds of interactions rarely occur in Paris or Seoul.

Advantages and disadvantages

The advantages of the *Excluder* approach to friendship are manifold and clear. There is a genuine sense of security and exclusivity that envelops these friendships, a sense that we are creating our own little social bubble and that nothing else matters. When I'm with my *Excluder* friends, there is a profound feeling of closeness and trust that can be very liberating, allowing me to feel totally at ease. There is no social demand to be entertaining or in any other way to put on a front for the sake of my friends. It can feel very comforting.

For an *Includer*, as someone who tends to be open and friendly to everyone, the exclusivity and closeness of the *Excluder* style can begin to feel confining after some time. One can get the impression that *Excluders* are "stuck" forever with their same circle of close friends.

Such an impression is unfair, and overextends the image of the *Excluder*. In my survey studies, for example, I never found a systematic difference in the duration of friendships between *Excluders* and *Includers*. Both groups seem to evidence an equal amount of turnover in their closest friendships. So, despite their tendency to act unfriendly toward strangers, *Excluders* can be quite open to making new friends. After all, at least a few of them became my friends! So I encourage you not to overextend the stereotypes I've created for friendships in France and South Korea.

Excluders:

*Behave differently toward friends versus people unknown to them

*Tend to be cold, "unfriendly," and wary toward strangers

*Feel much more secure in the company of a few close friends

*Employ a much more formal language with strangers

*For many Asians, strangers don't "exist," even when they are close by

*Have very well-developed social skills for closeness

*Tend to have low need for social approval from friends or strangers

*Enjoy spending extended periods of time with a close friend

*Can be offended by an *Includer* friend's tendency to talk to everyone

*Are less comfortable than *Includers* with meeting new people

---

Healthy adaptations

It's worth repeating that we all tend to adapt our style of friendship to fit the demands of the situation. This is especially true among young people today. The mobility of current employment patterns around the world strongly influences the nature of their close friendships.

Some years ago, my wife and I befriended a younger French couple who, because of his employer, have lived in four very different countries in the last 12 years. Such mobility almost requires an *Includer* approach to their friendships. To enjoy a satisfying social life in each of their new locales, they have had to be consistently open to new friendships. It has been interesting for us to watch them adapt and develop close and fulfilling friendships in each of these cultures.

> *Be courteous to all, but intimate with few, and let those few be well tried before you give them your confidence.*
>
> -George Washington

However, speaking in broad generalities, *Excluders* tend to have a harder time meeting new people and developing new friendships. The colder images they project don't facilitate socializing with strangers. They are simply less comfortable dealing with people they don't know well.

Looking ahead

Putting strangers at ease is a highly developed skill of *Includers* and the focus of the next chapter, which begins with a story about my irritation with the kindness of strangers.

Chapter 8

Includers: Good at first impressions

Charm is the ability to make someone think that both of you are quite wonderful.

–Source unknown

Going through my mail just hours after arriving home from my year-long sabbatical teaching at the American University in Paris, I found a letter from my local county government summoning me for jury duty the very next day. After a few phone calls, it became painfully clear there was no way to avoid my civic responsibility.

So early the next morning, jetlagged and exhausted, in the foulest of moods, I showed up at the courthouse jury waiting room along with dozens of other responsible citizens, waiting my turn to be called to duty. I came prepared with a book to read, Margaret Attwood's *Cat's Eye*, which I had begun on the plane trip home. I found it an absorbing read, allowing me to mentally escape my surroundings.

Gabby readers

I was engrossed in the story until I heard a voice, seeming like a distant echo in my semi-consciousness, even though it was coming from the woman sitting right next to me, asking, "I love Margaret Atwood. Is it good?"

"Excellent," I responded, hardly glancing up from the text.

"My husband started it and didn't like it," she continued.

"I really enjoy her work," responding curtly, hoping she would allow me to continue reading.

"It's on the NY Times bestseller list," said the man seated next to me on the other side.

"Yes it is," I responded, again curtly, frustrated at having read the same passage several times now.

"I've heard good things about Margaret Atwood," he began again, after just a moment's pause, "but I haven't read any of her stuff."

"Oh, she's great," the woman on the other side chimed back in, "My husband and I both read *The Handmaid's Tale* last year and loved it. Her stories can be rather dark and pessimistic, though. I have friends who don't like her at all."

How rude! I thought. Would these two gadflies simply shut up and leave me alone! Just when I thought things couldn't get worse, the woman seated directly in front of me turned around to offer her opinions on the matter. I couldn't believe it! Here I am minding my own business, and without the least provocation, I find myself in the middle of a conversation and trying hard not to participate.

The more they talked, the more I just sat and stewed, trying to think of things to say to put them in their place, or at least, get them to leave me in peace. How can I tell them how terribly rude they are? They are so inconsiderate. These people have no sensitivity or manners whatsoever!

Speech is civilization itself.

–Thomas Mann

It was at this point, the bit about "sensitivity or manners" when I realized I was the one lacking on both counts. Here I was, back in South Carolina—this is what people do in South Carolina. Everyone talks to everyone.

This is what I have always liked about Southerners, everyone is so open, friendly, and laidback. Just relax, Roger, I thought to myself. Close the book, join the conversation and enjoy it. And so I did.

"Yes," I added, "and this book is just as dark and pessimistic as her other works, but I love it. Her stories play on the less honorable sides of human nature." And from there, we proceeded to pass the rest of the morning, discussing everything each of us had read for the past six months.

It felt good to be home again!

Defining terms

USAers are a friendly lot, and Southerners are friendlier than most. Having just spent a year in a culture where talking so openly with total strangers in a setting such as this would have been much less likely, I initially found their friendly overtures invasive, presumptuous, and annoying.

This story exemplifies the *Includer* approach to one's social life. The term *Includers* refers to those who are open and friendly toward nearly everyone, even relative strangers. They think and feel quite differently about their closest friends, but these distinctions are seldom evident in their outward behavior. If a French or Korean acquaintance had happened in on that conversation, he or she would have thought we were all great friends, or at least, acquaintances. We laughed and talked, told stories, some rather personal, as if we had known each other for years, though I didn't even know their names.

Basic human contact — the meeting of eyes, the exchanging of words—is to the psyche what oxygen is to the brain.

-Martha Beck

This approach to one's social life contrasts sharply with that of the *Excluders* described in the last chapter, whose demeanor and behavior change quite dramatically when interacting with strangers versus close friends.

Ever since the time of de Tocqueville, outsiders have commented on the friendliness of USAers. Visitors to the U.S. initially find this overt friendliness very warm and welcoming, especially in the South.

Cross-cultural misunderstandings

However, their friendly *Includer* ways can also create confusion. Some newcomers to the U.S. think everyone they meet is interested in becoming a close friend when in fact they are simply being friendly. Eventually it all appears somewhat shallow, leading some to conclude USAers are incapable of real friendship.

This last conclusion is clearly unjustified. Based on my research and that of a growing number of others, USAers, even those who are extreme *Includers*, those who treat nearly everyone they encounter as a friend, even these individuals tend to have a small number of people they think of as close friends, who play important, supportive roles in their lives.

The problem is, this distinction is rarely obvious from outward appearances. They differentiate between close friends and "just friends" at cognitive and emotional levels, reflecting how they think and feel about them, but at the same time, they display roughly the same open and friendly behaviors toward everyone.

Adding to the confusion is how USAers employ the word "friend," which can refer to a broad range of acquaintances, from someone newly encountered to a friend one has held dear since childhood. All English-speaking cultures tend to use this term loosely, but this norm applies most clearly to USAers.

Wherever friendly paths intersect the whole world looks like home for a time.

–Hermann Hesse

USAer friendliness, however, extends well beyond semantics and shows up differently in various regions of the U.S. In the South, it tends to be an easy smile and warm eye contact, even among relative strangers. In New York City, it is more likely seen as a willingness to converse (or even argue) with anyone about most anything, depending on the situation. Regardless, at its core, it carries the expectation of reciprocity, that others will be similarly open to such exchanges as well.

A sad story

International students arriving on the Winthrop campus where I taught for 30 years were especially impressed with how open and friendly everyone was. In one way or another, when I broached the subject with students new to campus, most thought they were about to have the time of their lives with these friendly USAers.

As I mentioned in Chapter Five, I sought volunteers from among the international students to help me with my friendship research. I conducted confidential interviews with these volunteers from time to time, asking them about their friendship experiences. I was especially interested in their friendships with USAers, and how these friendships evolved over time.

One Brazilian student, having arrived in late August, thought he had finally made a USAer friend when a local student invited him home for Thanksgiving break. The Brazilian was thrilled. He got to experience first hand a very rich, traditional USAer Thanksgiving holiday, with all the festivities and trimmings of the season. He especially enjoyed the time he spent with his new friend and his family, and felt their friendship had grown much closer as they shared a variety of experiences, meeting the USAer's childhood friends and seeing all the places where he hung out as a high school student.

It is individuals that populate the world.

–Henry David Thoreau

But the Brazilian student was shocked and perplexed a day after they had returned when he passed his new friend walking across campus, who greeted him with a "Hi, how are you?" but then just kept going on his way to class, hardly pausing long enough for the Brazilian to respond. A similar incident happened the following day, with his new friend smiling broadly and acting friendly, but also passing him by with no more than a "What's up?"

To the Brazilian, there was clearly a problem.

He was convinced he had done something inappropriate over the weekend, something that had offended his new friend or his family in some way. He couldn't figure out why else his new friend would be brushing him off so curtly.

I learned about this incident when the Brazilian stopped by my office, asking me about several things he had said and done over the weekend, attempting to figure out how he had offended his hosts. He thought he had committed some sort of social or cultural faux pas. After a half hour or so of conversation, I came to the conclusion he had done nothing at all offensive. Rather, he and the USAer had different ideas about what it meant to be invited home for Thanksgiving.

I never met the USAer student in question, but my guess is he invited the Brazilian simply to give him someplace to go over the break. It was a friendly gesture and probably nothing more, consistent with the USAer tradition to celebrate Thanksgiving in large gatherings of family and friends. Perhaps he even felt sorry for the Brazilian, I don't know.

Regardless, the Brazilian student had read more into this gesture than the USAer student intended. I suspect that in Brazil, being invited into someone's home is interpreted as a gesture of closeness, but for the USAer, he was just being friendly.

Some happy stories

I should point out that I did see friendships develop between international and USAer students while at Winthrop. International students who remained on campus for a year or more were much more likely to end up with USAer friends, and the USAers in these friendships were often students I knew, because they attended International Center events. These were students with international interests, who had either studied abroad or were planning to do so.

I was always quite curious about these international students and their friendships with USAers, and tried to interview as many of them as I could. They were often students who were fully and comfortably adapted to USAer culture. Most, but not all, saw their friendships with USAers as different from those back home, and many could even articulate the nature of these differences, all of which nourished my thinking about these matters.

Although this was long before I began using the term, a few of them could talk at length about the advantages of living in a culture of *Includers*. They found it comforting to be among such friendly people, people who readily socialize with nearly everyone they encounter in their everyday lives. It left them believing that the U.S. is a safe place and that most people can be trusted, which, because of our emphasis on crime in the news media, was often the opposite of the expectations they arrived with.

The greatest happiness of life is the conviction that we are loved.

–Victor Hugo

If you put yourself in their shoes and reflect on it for a minute, when strangers greet you as you encounter them, if they smile, look you in the eye and say "hi," it is a kind of affirmation of your own existence. You are a person, a human being, and others acknowledge your presence in a positive way. When such experiences occur regularly, it produces feelings of warmth, acceptance and security, even though the source of these feelings comes from total strangers. Over the last decade, relationship researchers have begun to study the benefits of what they refer to as "peripheral relationships."

I especially notice this aspect of USAer culture when coming home after having been abroad for an extended period of time. In a very subtle way, these affirmations can be reassuring, leaving me with optimistic notions about my fellow human beings.

The kindness of strangers

Much has been made in USAer social psychology of the "bystander effect," where several people witness someone in desperate need of help but no one raises a finger, as in the infamous 1960s case of Kitty Genovese who was murdered in her New York City neighborhood while many allegedly heard and watched the entire tragedy without calling the police.

> *Men who have real friends are less easy to manage or 'get at,' harder for good authorities to correct or for bad authorities to corrupt.*
>
> –C.S. Lewis

The bystander effect is shocking and noteworthy primarily because it runs contrary to the USAer expectation that others are looking out for their welfare. Would the bystander effect be as relevant in a culture where anyone I don't know personally simply "doesn't exist" as described in the last chapter? USAers wouldn't study such things if they didn't feel some responsibility for their fellow human beings, even complete strangers.

The bystander effect makes for an interesting cross-cultural comparison. As explained in Chapter Five, USAers are generally less comfortable taking care of, or being taken care of by their close friends. They tend to avoid such dependencies. However, when it comes to total strangers, the picture seems to get reversed, and USAers appear to have more concern for them than would be the case in many other cultures of the world. It is a natural outgrowth of the general friendliness that is shown to everyone, friends, acquaintances, and even strangers.

Includers and their close friends

A key point I would like you to keep in mind is that despite their indiscriminant friendliness, *Includers* tend to think of themselves as having a few close, meaningful friendships. My friendship surveys have characteristically been quite long, asking lots of personal questions about one particular friend they've selected as the focus of their survey responses. At the very end, after they have had ample time to think about this friendship and what it means to them, I ask them to indicate the number of people they consider as close friends. Without exception, respondents in the U.S. have always indicated the smallest number of close friends compared to other cultures I've studied.

My father always used to say that when you die, if you've got five real friends, then you've had a great life.

–Lee Iacocca

This finding stands in stark contrast with mainstream thinking in cross-cultural psychology, which holds that USAers have only superficial relationships with a large number of friends. I've been gratified in recent years that other researchers asking the same questions have received similar results.

USAers feel and think about their closest friends quite differently than they do others who are mere acquaintances. They care deeply about their closest friends, and in return, these friendships provide the USAer with multiple benefits, both in terms of physical health and psychological wellbeing. We will explore these findings in detail in Chapter Eleven. For now, the point is that this research demonstrates that USAers tend to cultivate much more than just superficial, inconsequential friendships.

Social skills for the superficial

Nevertheless, they behave in a friendly manner toward most people in their environments, and this approach to their social lives requires its own set of social skills. Just as the *Excluders* discussed in the last chapter have specially developed social skills for closeness that allow them to spend extended periods of time with close friends, *Includers* cultivate what have been called "social skills for superficial interactions," which help them in their day-to-day social lives.

Includers are comfortable carrying on conversations with relative strangers while in the waiting room for jury duty, for example, or while standing in line at the grocery store. Their ready smiles, warm eye contact and open manner facilitate these interactions. They have developed talents for putting others at ease, even triggering in them a tendency to reciprocate their advances. They know how to bring out agreeable exchanges with others, and everyone feels at ease.

If you are like most USAers, you often complain about your poor memories for people's names. However, the typical USAer's ability to call people by name shortly after meeting them in settings like a cocktail party often leaves people from other cultures in awe. I have heard this comment often from international visitors: USAers are quite good at meeting new people, calling them by name and making them feel at ease.

I keep my friends as misers do their treasure, because, of all the things granted us by wisdom, none is greater or better than friendship.

–Pietro Aretino

For anyone seeking a sort of manual for developing these social skills for superficial interactions, may I recommend the classic Dale Carnegie book, *How to Win Friends and Influence People*. To me, this is the quintessential guide for perfecting *Includer* social skills. While it has little to do with friendship as we are using the term here, it has much to do with being friendly, and everything to do with influencing people and becoming an economic success. This explains its enormous popularity in the business community, even today, 75 years after it was published.

I nod to a passing stranger, and the stranger nods back, and two human beings go off, feeling a little less anonymous.

–Robert Brault

The skills taught in this book parallel those of a successful *Includer*. How to make a good first impression, be welcome wherever you go, make others feel important, call people by name, be a good listener, encourage others to talk about themselves, use praise, avoid arguments, show respect to others, and see the other's point of view. There is even an entire chapter on the importance of smiling!

These social skills in action

For the typical USAer, the development of these social skills begins very early and they are already well established in adolescence, as depicted in the following anecdote.

A couple of summers after my sabbatical year in Paris, I hosted a French couple along with their 14 year-old daughter for their first vacation in the U.S. At one point, in an attempt to entertain the child and the adults at the same time, I took them to a local amusement park where we found ourselves waiting in long lines to board some intensely thrilling ride that lasted about 90 seconds.

There were lots of other adolescents in the park, many of them about the age of their daughter and she was obviously very curious about them. In one of these interminable lines, there were two girls and two boys waiting immediately in front of us. It became clear that the girls were friends and the boys were friends but the two pairs didn't know each other.

Youth! There is nothing like youth!

-Oscar Wilde

Initially, they ignored each other except for occasional furtive glances. As the line crept along, however, things became more interesting. I think all of us were fascinated, watching their giggling, mutual flirtations, and occasional exchanges of comments. The boarding time was slowly approaching, and the ride had separate cars, each accommodating four people, two on each side.

As the four teenagers entered their car, the two boys sat on one side and the girls facing them on the other, but seconds before they lowered the bars that held them in their seats, one boy and one girl in each pair got up and switched places, leaving them as two couples. They all giggled heartily, and off they went as the ride took them laughing and screaming up into the air for their 90 seconds of thrills!

My friends' daughter turned to me and quipped, "That same drama would have taken six months to unfold in France!" which gave us all a big laugh. I offer this anecdote as an example of the *Includer* social skills at work.

All of our current versions of social media have greatly facilitated meeting like-minded strangers, and these phenomena are having a major impact in *Excluder* cultures, where interacting with strangers has traditionally been very challenging. It has never been much of a problem for USAers.

While *Includers* are at ease in most social situations, they are much less comfortable spending extended periods of time with a friend, even a close friend. They have difficulty dealing with the closeness that stems from prolonged contact. They often find, for example, that best friends don't make for good college roommates or even business partners, a maxim that would not apply to *Excluder* cultures of the world.

Wanting to be liked

Also unlike the *Excluders*, *Includers* tend to be motivated by a strong desire to be liked by everyone, even those with whom they are not well acquainted. They apply their highly developed social skills for the superficial throughout their daily lives, as they interact with people who are well-known or complete strangers. At work, with neighbors or friends, no matter where they find themselves, they are always exercising these social skills.

If others return their smiles, their friendly banter, their attempts at charm and humor, it leaves them feeling good about themselves. Indeed, their identities and self-esteem, even their moods, are based in part on employing these skills successfully. All social interactions are opportunities for positive feedback. They are constantly hungry for and sensitive to signs of approval, even from strangers.

Conversely, they are bothered when receiving negative or disapproving feedback, even when such reactions come from people they don't know. A cross word from a checkout clerk at a grocery store, for example, can be upsetting for hours after the incident. It would represent a failure in the exercise of their social skills for superficial interactions and therefore a blow, perhaps a relatively minor one in the overall scheme of things, but nevertheless a blow to their self-confidence. They would wonder what they did to offend the clerk or why they were deserving of such "abuse." They will try to excuse themselves by assuming the clerk was having a bad day or simply has a negative disposition. But such excuses do not prevent them from being bothered.

> *Lead the life that will make you kindly and friendly to everyone about you, and you will be surprised what a happy life you will lead.*
>
> –Charles M. Schwab

On the other hand, for an *Excluder*, people who make clear distinctions between those they know well and those they don't, a cross word from a checkout clerk would probably not even gain their attention, and if the slight were noticed, it would likely have little effect. It simply doesn't matter.

A case study

So what happens when an *Includer* and an *Excluder* try to forge a friendship with each other? In this composite case, based on stories I witnessed over the years working with international students, problems in communications will be obvious from the very beginning.

Marie-Pierre from Montpellier, France, and Sarah from Fort Lauderdale, Florida were newly arriving graduate students, Marie-Pierre an MBA student and Sarah beginning a graduate program in school psychology. They met through an ad Sarah had posted outside the housing office indicating she was seeking a roommate for her two bedroom apartment. Sarah was anxious to find someone since she couldn't afford the rent on her own.

Sticking to cultural stereotypes, I will designate Sarah as the *Includer* and Marie-Pierre as the *Excluder*, although it is important to remember it is not difficult to find USAer *Excluders* and French *Includers*. Despite my penchant for playing on stereotypes, we must always guard against over-thinking these generalities.

The two met by chance when Sarah spied Marie-Pierre reading her ad outside the housing office. She approached her with a smile and a sales pitch about the amenities of the apartment and how nice it would be for them to be roommates. Marie-Pierre found Sarah warm, charming and funny, and they decided to ride over to look at the place.

Assumptions are the termites of relationships.

–Henry Winkler

Sarah's first impressions of Marie-Pierre weren't completely positive. Marie-Pierre appeared distracted, with tired eyes that always seemed to be looking off to the side when they spoke. Sarah tried to put her at ease by asking about her hometown, her family and why she decided to come to this university. Marie-Pierre gave short answers that weren't very revealing and she didn't ask Sarah anything in return except for the rent arrangements and other issues related to the apartment. Sarah attributed Marie-Pierre's lack of warmth to jetlag and perhaps her wariness of being in an unfamiliar environment. She also seemed to be struggling with her English.

From Marie-Pierre's point of view, she found Sarah instantly likeable. She seemed warm and caring and Marie-Pierre felt lucky to have met her, thinking she would make a good roommate and she was excited about the possibility of making a USAer friend. Marie-Pierre agreed to move in and Sarah, quite relieved, helped move her things since Marie-Pierre didn't own a car. The first few weeks went well, although both were quite busy with school. They each liked to cook, and on several occasions they shared dinners together, drinking wine, and talking late into the evening, often bemoaning the lack of men in their lives, an unfortunate but inevitable side effect of being overworked graduate students.

These long and personal conversations led Marie-Pierre to thinking she and Sarah were becoming close friends. Sarah told her all about her recent break-up with her college boyfriend. Sarah liked Marie-Pierre, although some of her personal habits irritated her. Marie-Pierre tended to lag when it was her turn to do dishes and always left hair all over the bathroom sink and shower. But these things were minor, and Sarah never mentioned them. Overall, she was slowly growing to like Marie-Pierre.

Sarah kept urging Marie-Pierre to invite some of her fellow MBA students over for a party, especially since the Business School had a surplus of single men. Marie-Pierre said she didn't know her fellow students well enough to do that, but she did mention that she was invited to a party of fellow MBA students and she would feel much better about going if Sarah went with her. Sarah was elated and both of them looked forward to the event.

When the party was over, each had very different reactions. Sarah had the time of her life—laughing and talking with everyone, drinking just a bit too much, but in the end, meeting lots of new people, including some guys with real potential. She also liked going out with Marie-Pierre whose French accent seemed to charm everyone. She was impressed with how much fun Marie-Pierre could be at a party.

For Marie-Pierre, the party was unlike any she had ever known. Everyone seemed bent on drinking as much as possible, some of the guys were playing video games, others watching basketball on TV, and no one was dancing. She was worried for Sarah who drank too much, talked loudly and inappropriately to everyone, especially the guys. Although they went to the party together, Marie-Pierre thought Sarah mostly ignored her, except to occasionally mock her accent, which got laughs from everyone. The experience caused her to rethink their developing friendship.

Case analysis

Viewing this scenario from the *Includer-Excluder* perspective, upon first meeting, Sarah was put off by Marie-Pierre's lack of eye contact and reticent manner. Marie-Pierre found Sarah's warmth and friendliness very reassuring and felt they could be good roommates and perhaps good friends as well. Marie-Pierre was charmed by Sarah's social skills for superficial exchanges making her feel instantly at ease.

Sarah's tendency to share her problems and talk about personal matters left Marie-Pierre believing they were becoming close friends. Later though, Marie-Pierre grew disappointed that Sarah didn't seem to value their friendship. They had agreed to go to the party together, but Sarah mostly ignored her, while saying overly personal things to everyone else. Sarah's mocking her accent and other subtle indicators left her feeling there was some hidden tension between them, that Sarah was upset about something but not telling her directly. All this left Marie-Pierre wondering if Sarah was even capable of close friendship, because of, in the words of the cross-cultural theorists, her lack of social skills for closeness.

It is worth noting that both Marie-Pierre and Sarah had friendly intentions, both wanted friendship. Each had their own ways of expressing those feelings. Their communication lapses and misunderstandings stemmed from their differing notions about what it means to be a good friend.

Includers:

*Project an open friendly demeanor to nearly everyone

*Treat close friends and casual acquaintances alike

*Their friendliness may appear shallow and insincere to *Excluders*

*Feel/think differently about close friends, but this doesn't show

*Tend to use the term "friend" very loosely

*Others may interpret their friendliness as a desire for friendship

*Find friendliness of strangers reassuring; people can be trusted

---

*Feel somewhat responsible for the welfare of strangers

*Have well-developed "social skills for superficial interactions"

*Are uncomfortable spending prolonged time with friends

*Feel high need for social approval from everyone, even strangers

Reviewing the four styles so far

It may be helpful for you at this point if I review our progress just a bit. In Chapters Four, Five, and Six, I distinguished between *Interveners* and *Independents*. *Interveners* feel a greater duty and responsibility to take care of their friends, and do so by actively intervening in their lives when appropriate. *Independents* respect each other's autonomy and demonstrate their friendship by sharing important personal information and by providing moral support during difficult times.

In Chapters Seven and Eight, I described how cultures differ in the ways they behave toward close friends versus strangers. *Excluders* make strong distinctions between the two, behaving formally and often suspiciously toward strangers, while acting and feeling much more relaxed and unrestrained around close friends. *Includers* behave in an outwardly friendly manner with most people they encounter, although cognitively and emotionally, they think of very few people as close friends.

Looking ahead

The next two chapters focus more specifically on how we think about our closest friendships, in realistic, sometimes critical terms versus a more idealized, always-supportive approach. I begin the next chapter with a story about getting caught in the middle of a heated argument between two *Realist* friends.

Chapter 9

Realists: Telling it like it is

A true friend stabs you in the front.

–Oscar Wilde

Have you ever gotten caught in the middle of a heated argument between two friends? That is where I found myself one bright sunny day in downtown Seoul. And to make matters worse, I couldn't even understand what they were arguing about. Let me explain.

Since cross-sex friendships are somewhat unusual in South Korea, whenever I got together with my psychiatrist friend, it was often with another colleague or in a family setting with her husband and two boys. In this way, it was clear to everyone we were simply colleagues and friends. When we met for lunches, she would often invite along a professional colleague or two who would have interesting perspectives on my study of friendship. On one such occasion, our lunch companion turned out to be a female colleague who was also one of her best friends.

I wanted to be invisible

The three of us met in my friend's office, and while we were descending the elevator on the way to the parking deck, the two of them got into an argument. They began quarrelling about something or other, I couldn't tell what, since my Korean was still too feeble at that point to even get the gist of their conflict. But voices were raised, they exchanged pointed statements at a rapid pace, and there were lots of "an-yea-oh's," the Korean expression for "no."

I was beginning to feel ill at ease, concerned that my presence was complicating their need to deal with the disagreement.

When we arrived at the parking deck, her friend got in a separate car—apparently the plan was for her to meet us at the restaurant. So I found myself alone with my friend in her car and I tried delicately to ask about the nature of their argument. To my surprise, she had no idea what I was talking about!

Instead of suppressing conflicts, specific channels could be created to make this conflict explicit, and specific methods could be set up by which the conflict is resolved.

–Albert Low

I witnessed several similar episodes during my year in South Korea, situations where friends were having conflict, or at least, what seemed to me to be conflict, only to learn later that wasn't the case. In this example, my friend and her friend were deciding on the driving arrangements, because each had plans after lunch that took them in differing directions. She said they talked about which would be better, one car or two. Yes, they disagreed on how to proceed, but she insisted they weren't the least bit upset with each other.

If you have learned how to disagree without being disagreeable, then you have discovered the secret of getting along -- whether it be business, family relations, or life itself.

–Bernard Meltzer

As we made our way through the busy streets of Seoul, my friend began to laugh at me, politely mind you, but she was clearly amused at my concern about their "argument." She had spent lots of time in the U.S., and she explained that Koreans tend to be more "frank with each other" compared to USAers. Then she added with a broad, somewhat mocking smile, "I like Americans, they are so sensitive and so polite!"

Her comment didn't fit my cultural stereotype of USAers, but when it comes to how we interact with close friends, perhaps she had a point. My observations, like this one between my friend and her friend, along with my research results have led me to conclude that what would qualify as "conflict" for a USAer could simply be a "discussion" among Koreans. In this case, a discussion aimed at solving a transportation issue.

Defining terms

My friend's exchange with her friend exemplifies what I call the *Realist* approach to friendship. I will contrast it with the *Idealist* approach in the next chapter, which tends to be more characteristic of USAers. These two styles of friendship have much to do with how we think about our close friends. In the case of the *Realists*, as the name implies, they tend to see their friends realistically, more objectively, including both their attractive and less attractive qualities in equal measure.

On confidential surveys I administered while in South Korea, respondents would rate their close friends very positively, but rarely as positively as USAers would. These more complex pictures among Korean friends would also come out in my informal interviews. Close friends could be described as sloppy dressers, unreliable or quick tempered, in addition to being intelligent, loveable and kind, with a great sense of humor. *Realists* tend not to sugarcoat things. Koreans would consistently rate a survey item such as "My friend would do almost anything for me" lower than would USAers.

Only your real friends will tell you when your face is dirty.

–Sicilian Proverb

(There are daunting methodological complications with making these kinds of comparisons across cultures. If you are curious about such things, I encourage you to spend some time with the appendix where I delve into the challenges and methodologies of doing cross-cultural research.)

In presentations I have given to USAers about the *Realist* style of friendship, I have often used the analogy of sibling relationships. That is, close friendships among *Realists* resemble how we commonly think about our own siblings in the U.S. The analogy works best if we think about how we dealt with our siblings when we were children or young adults.

When it comes to our siblings, most of us would say we love them dearly. In fact, we typically care a lot about them and want what is best for them. At the same time, it would not be unusual for us to point out their faults or areas where we clash. We tend to appraise our siblings even-handedly, or in terms of this discussion, we see them realistically.

This is how I perceive many *Realist* Koreans when they talk about their closest friends. They weren't hesitant to mention experiences where their friends were annoying or a burden. It was clear they cared deeply about their friends. But it was also clear they didn't view their friends with rose-colored glasses.

Speech has been given to man to disguise his thoughts.

–Charles-Maurice de Talleyrand

The *Realist* and *Idealist* styles of friendship primarily reflect how we think about our friends, and thus, the differences between these two styles are not readily observable, except when examining their responses on confidential surveys. However, one area where we can see a clear difference is in how they talk to each other. *Realists* tend to be much more frank, direct, even confrontational in their ways of interacting with each other as friends, compared to the *Idealists* who prefer playing a more supportive role.

Getting the bigger picture

To get a better grasp of what I'm speaking of, I need to provide some context for the Korean frankness with their friends. This idea stands in stark contrast with the more general cross-cultural literature on social behaviors, where Koreans have the reputation of being far less direct or confrontational in their communication patterns when compared to USAers. Koreans, for example, have a much harder time saying "no" in response to a request from another person, especially if that person is a superior. They have a hard time saying "no" even if they know they can't realistically fulfill the request.

Communication experts have studied the various forms of directness and indirectness in speech patterns in cultures around the world. According to their thinking, USAers are generally considered the direct ones, getting right to the point, rather than beating around the bush. USAers value clarity. If they ask a question, they want a direct answer, not an oblique one, which employs flowery analogies or asks a competing question.

Many cross-cultural communication studies focus on the international business community, where finding agreement, making deals and signing contracts—everyday occurrences in the world of global business—require communicating with a high degree of precision and clarity. According to these studies, in the U.S., business people who are relative strangers can come together, shake hands, sit down for a bit of polite chitchat, and then go directly to work. If their business dealings are successful, their collaborations will continue, and at some point, they may become friends, going on golf outings or socializing with each other's families. Their approach to these things seems to value the maxim of "business before pleasure."

> *All faults may be forgiven of him who has perfect candor.*
>
> –Walt Whitman

In less direct cultures of the world, this scenario would be reversed. One would need to build a strong and trusting relationship, with lots of dinners, perhaps months or even years of courting a potential business deal, and only then can they collaborate on some sort of project. Perhaps the maxim for them should be "pleasure before business" or at least, "relationships before business."

A German story

I'll provide another example, gleaned from the work of Edward and Mildred Hall in their book entitled *Understanding Cultural Differences*. Suppose a German was making a persuasive speech in a business, academic, or political setting. He or she would most likely begin by providing the historical and cultural background for the argument, even before revealing the argument itself. Lots of past and current evidence supporting the main point would be sequentially and systematically presented without explicitly stating the main point.

> *Better pointed bullets than pointed speeches.*
>
> –Otto von Bismarck

As the presentation progresses, the persuasive arguments would accumulate until eventually the climax would be reached which would be the main point of the argument itself. The groundwork for the case is laid so elaborately one is left with little choice but to accept the validity of the main argument.

According to the Halls, the typical USAer making the same speech would employ a very different tactic. No matter the context, even in the case of a eulogy for someone who has died, USAers love to start out with some sort of humorous story. This is intended to break the ice and develop rapport with the listeners, another example of their "social skills for the superficial" described in the last chapter.

Once everyone has had a relaxing laugh, the next step is to state the purpose of the presentation; that is, USAers tend to go directly to the main point. No historical background, no development of the context, no long sequence of preparatory arguments—simply and directly, wham bang, hitting the audience with the main argument. And then they go on to explain, defend, and reinforce the main point with convincing evidence and arguments.

Speak properly, and in as few words as you can, but always plainly; for the end of speech is not ostentation, but to be understood.

-William Penn

These are examples of the communicative directness of USAers when compared to many other cultures of the world. East Asians are often cited as the clearest examples of indirectness. Despite the example just given, Germans are also generally considered as quite direct in most communication contexts.

Direct friends

My research and that of others lead me to suspect much of this gets reversed when it comes to the communication patterns among close friends. In this case, the Koreans are generally far more direct in how they talk with friends compared to USAers. When it comes to their closest friends, Koreans feel such a level of comfort, they have such a sense of confidence in the relationship, they experience little need for the politics and politeness of indirectness.

I should caution this directness among friends would not apply to all topics or situations. Whenever there is a public display or the potential for a public display among friends, they tend to follow the more prevailing norm of indirectness in their friendship exchanges.

But often, my Korean friends were breathtakingly direct with me. In fact, their well-intentioned criticisms of various things I had done seemed quite harsh by USAer standards. This more direct style of talk reflects how *Realists* think about their friends. And herein lies the greatest benefit of having a *Realist* friend—the relationship feels very genuine, more trusting, and at the risk of overusing the term, more "real."

This would apply to any interactions between you and a *Realist* friend—you can count on any feedback you get, positive or negative, as honest and forthright. It didn't take me long to figure this out, and I fully appreciate this aspect of my more *Realist* friends.

If you've been paying close attention to my arguments so far, you may have noticed a contradiction in what I'm saying here. Recall back to Chapter Six, I talked about my Korean psychiatrist friend's indirectness in her conversations with me. And now I'm arguing that when it comes to their close friendships, it is the Koreans who are far more direct than we are.

There is nothing like the razor sharp tongue of a good friend to cut through the lies we tell ourselves.

–Laura Moncur

My explanation, simply stated, is that I don't think she ever treats me as she would a Korean friend. She has had extensive experience living in the U.S. and dealing with USAers, and she defers to our cultural norms when it concerns our friendship. My other Korean friend and others I became close to while living in South Korea were all much more frank in their interactions with me, more in line with what would be expected among *Realist* friends.

Candor is the brightest gem of criticism.

–Benjamin Disraeli

Others have made the observation that Koreans can be quite frank and direct, even critical, as part of their interactions with close friends. Communications researchers Yong-Ok Yum and Daniel J. Canary make reference to the "negative communication style" among Koreans in a chapter devoted to close relationships in a book entitled *Maintaining Relationships through Communications*.

I tend not to see this style of communication as "negative." Rather, I think of it the way my Korean psychiatrist friend first explained to me: Koreans are simply more frank in how they talk to their closest friends. They tend to be more *Realist* in the ways they think about and interact with them. *Realists* feel less inhibited about disagreeing, arguing or pointing out where the friend is going wrong, and they tend to see this as normal friend behavior.

It is also worth noting that *Realist* Koreans don't see such behavior as constituting conflict. To me, it looks like, sounds like, feels like they're having serious conflict. To them, it apparently doesn't feel that way, and this is evident in my surveys and interviews. To them, it's just what *Realist* friends do.

Those disagreeable French

The French, too, are not shy about disagreeing with their close friends, although this tendency is exemplified most clearly in the realm of ideas—having heated arguments about some important issue is a sort of verbal sport, for which the French are famous...or is it infamous! They see such disputes as interesting and fun, just the kind of thing friends like to do.

> The people to fear are not those who disagree with you, but those who disagree with you and are too cowardly to let you know.
>
> -Napoleon Bonaparte

Parents I know in Paris, for example, had recently met their daughter's fiancé for the first time and I happened to be there for the occasion. I found the young man charming and intelligent, and he was obviously deeply in love with their daughter. After the young couple left, one remark of the parents struck me. Among other comments, the father said he found the young man a bit "too agreeable." Apparently, in the discussions we were having about issues of the day, he didn't stake out a point of view and argue his case sufficiently. I simply can't imagine any USAer parents I know making such a comment, that their potential son-in-law was "too agreeable."

To sum up, even though cross-cultural theorists have traditionally seen USAers as the direct ones in their communications with others, and Koreans as an example of indirectness, I argue just the opposite applies to close friendships, where Korean frankness with their close friends has been documented in the research literature.

Saving face

There is perhaps another related area where close friendships don't fit the more generic cultural stereotypes studied by cross-cultural experts: This concerns the concept of "face."

Cross-cultural researchers refer to some, mostly collectivist, cultures as being "face cultures," since they place a lot of emphasis on maintaining harmony in all social situations. In general, to prevent embarrassment or the loss of face, one should avoid disagreeing, correcting, providing public negative feedback, or, as I mentioned above, even saying "no" to rather innocuous questions. Any kind of disagreement can cause a loss of face, especially when the receiver of this disagreement has higher social status.

Opposition is true friendship.

-William Blake

One can also risk losing face if one appears incompetent, doesn't seem appropriately prepared for circumstances, admits a mistake or even asks for help. People living in face cultures have developed elaborate social schemes to deal with problems or disagreements indirectly, allowing everyone to save face and maintain harmony, which is critical for everyday social functioning.

All of this applies quite clearly in South Korea. To save face, Koreans will often answer a request affirmatively, even when they won't be fulfilling the request. During my year there, I learned various ways to determine when a "yes" really means "yes" and not "maybe yes," "probably not," or just plain "no." Usually this involved some hesitancy or indirectness in the response.

Travel teaches tolerance.

-Benjamin Disraeli

For example, I took my printer in for repairs and asked the shop owner whether it would be ready by that evening. He said "yes" but this response came after a brief pause during which he did what we expats fondly referred to as "sucking noodles." That is, his saying "yes" was preceded by a brief, sharp inhalation, with lips slightly parted, as if he were sucking noodles into his mouth.

I recognized the signs. I knew this meant my printer was unlikely to be ready that evening and I made plans to work around my need for it.

To a USAer, this may sound like a convoluted way to communicate. They value directness and efficiency, and are generally not concerned with maintaining face. The dictum is one of "say what you mean and mean what you say." On the other hand, I met many USAers living in Korea who had readily adapted to this norm and saw the advantages of maintaining interpersonal harmony.

Examples of the USAer lack of concern about face can be seen in academic, business, and professional settings, where it is perfectly acceptable to provide negative feedback to someone who hasn't performed up to expectations. Even though the receiver of this feedback may not like it, the practice is common and most experts consider it a normal management strategy.

There may be other cultures that are even less face-oriented than USAers. If there were an international "no" scale, for example, I think East Asians would probably have the hardest time saying "no," the French would have the easiest and USAers would score somewhere in between. This assertion is more than just a conjecture, since if you read the Appendix to this book, you will learn that the methods used in cross-cultural research require one to statistically correct for such cultural response biases.

Friends and face

Despite these very well established ideas regarding face and non-face cultures, I suspect the picture gets reversed when it comes to our interaction patterns with close friends. In this case, it is the USAers who are concerned with face, with maintaining harmony in their closest friendships.

Even the utmost goodwill and harmony and practical kindness are not sufficient for friendship, for friends do not live in harmony merely, as some say, but in melody.

–Henry David Thoreau

And it is the Koreans, traditionally seen as a face culture, who are less concerned with this issue in their closest friendships. At least the *Realists* among them see the issue of face as having less relevance for the conduct of their friendships. As my psychiatrist friend commented, Korean friends can be very frank with each other, in this case, "saying what they mean, and meaning what they say."

The strength of their friendship allows them the liberty to disagree directly and strongly, to be critical, or in other ways confront a friend about things he or she may have said or done. I eventually grew to appreciate this friendship norm. When my friends were telling me in no uncertain terms what they thought I needed to know, it began to actually feel "warm," like there was a strong bond of trust between us. I find my USAer friends rarely speak to me so frankly, and that is okay too.

How close are the friends?

In Chapter Five, I mentioned the paradoxical but pervasive finding that on measures of relationship closeness, people often rate their friendships as closer in individualist or *Independent* cultures compared to collectivist or *Intervener* cultures. I was making the point that each style of friendship has its own way of defining what it means to have a close friend, and that it is difficult to make such comparisons across cultures.

For *Interveners*, feelings of closeness stem from their interdependence—friends depend on each other, they take care of each other in multiple ways both emotionally and by actually doing things for each other, by intervening when necessary. For *Independents*, feelings of closeness arise from simply having fun together, enjoying their time away from the competitive world of work, or by serving as a good listener and offering words of encouragement when a friend has a problem.

Realists similarly score lower on measures of relationship closeness even though this style of friendship is associated with collectivist cultures where people are generally thought to have much closer relationship compared to individualist cultures where people are raised to stand on their own. Looking carefully at how social scientists measure relationship closeness will provide some insight into this paradox, and at the same time, help us understand what it means to be a good *Realist* friend.

> To measure the man, measure his heart.
>
> –Malcolm Forbes

There are lots of different measures of relationship closeness, but they all have in common the fact that they are based on self-reports, how people rate themselves on surveys, questionnaires, interviews, or in diaries where they keep a record of all their interactions with friends over a period of time. No one can rate how we feel about a friend for us. Since that is the case, all these measures echo how we think about friendship, how we define what it means to be a good friend.

Realists have their own particular ideas about what it means to be a close friend. One category of measures of relationship closeness is called "relationship maintenance," which refers to how we maintain, enhance, or affirm our relationships with significant others in their lives. Typical items on these measures include things like being open and willing to communicate with the friend, keeping a positive approach during interactions, being supportive and reassuring to the friend, and avoiding negative issues or unfriendly behaviors.

Some of these issues—keeping a positive approach, being reassuring, and avoiding negative issues—are not aspects of close friendships that are highly valued by *Realists*. They don't see it as their duty to boost the egos of their friends. It simply doesn't feel right, like the kind of thing friends would do.

In the *Realist* version of a close friendship, friends can speak openly and frankly, even to the point of sometimes confronting each other about minor everyday matters but also about important or sensitive issues—things the friend might find difficult to accept. These are friendly behaviors. Such talk is evidence of trust and closeness, of a high level of mutual involvement in each other's lives. They represent a *Realist's* definition of what it means to be a close friend.

Those who venture to criticize us perform a remarkable act of friendship, for to undertake to wound and offend a man for his own good is to have a healthy love for him.

-Michel de Montaigne

There is still another reason why *Realists* may score lower on measures of relationship maintenance, which provides an additional insight into how they think about friendship. They don't conceive of friendships as something that has to be actively "maintained" to ensure their survival. To some degree, *Realists* can take their friendships for granted. They assume their friends will always be their friends.

This assumption is based on the belief that fate plays a critical role in all close relationships, including friendships. *Realists* tend to believe they are predestined to have the friends they do. In Korea, this concept is referred to as *yon*, and in China, the equivalent is *yuan*. British cross-cultural researcher Robin Goodwin and his colleagues have done interesting studies showing that these concepts dominate how one thinks about friendship in Asian cultures.

Because of the distance, I rarely see my Korean friends these days. But when I do, on nearly every occasion, they will mention the fact that fate (or karma, or destiny, or divine providence) has brought us together as good friends.

Since one's friendships are assumed as givens among *Realists*, something over which one has little choice or control, it makes little sense to actively maintain them by being reassuring, avoiding negative issues, or keeping a positive approach in one's interactions. For the *Realist*, these are not typical friend behaviors. They might seem more like inappropriate flattery, something a true friend would see through at once.

Flatterers look like friends, as wolves like dogs.

–George Chapman

Given all of these complications about notions of friendship closeness, I think it is best to conclude, as I have done repeatedly now, that it is extremely difficult to make such inferences across cultures. Each feels close to their friends in very different ways. And there are too many counterarguments to conclude, as many have, that USAers are not oriented toward close friendships.

Realists:

*Do not hold idealized notions of their closest friends

*Think about friends as having both positive and negative traits

*On surveys, do not rate traits of friends as highly as do *Idealists*

*Don't see it as their role to boost the egos of their closest friends

*Are comfortable speaking directly and frankly with a close friend

*Can disagree strongly with a friend without it feeling like a conflict

*Are less concerned about issues of face with their closest friends

*Rate friends less highly, thus lowering scores on relationship closeness

*See friendships as predestined; thus not needing "maintenance"

Telling on myself

When it comes to my own friends, I tend to be a rather typical USAer, generally preferring the *Independent* and *Includer* styles of friendship. However, when it comes to the topic of this chapter, I see myself as more of a *Realist*, especially when it comes to speaking frankly with close friends. I am generally not shy about confronting or disagreeing with friends, even on important issues.

One incident a few summers back brought home the realization that I may be deluding myself. My wife and I were hosting a young Russian student in our home—she was staying in the U.S. for the summer on a temporary work-study visa. One night, we invited friends over for dinner and through the course of the evening, lubricated with a few libations, we engaged in some lively discussions, one of the most contentious ones concerning the politics of the day.

> *Don't make friends who are comfortable to be with. Make friends who will force you to lever yourself up.*
>
> -Thomas J. Watson

It was an election year, and there were strong and opposing feelings on both the candidates and the issues. Voices were raised, tempers flared and strong opinions were expressed, not an uncommon occurrence on such occasions. People were passionate about their points of view, and our conversations (and perhaps the wine) served to liberate those strong feelings.

After our guests had gone home and we were together cleaning up the dishes, I asked the Russian student what she thought of the evening. She made some polite and complimentary comments, but I pressed her specifically about what she thought of our discussion on the election.

Her response floored me. She explained how impressed she was that we all remained so calm and polite, even when talking about such difficult topics. "If this dinner had taken place in my home," she remarked, "there would have been an all-out shouting match, or worse!" So much for my personal notions about not fitting the USAer stereotype on this count.

Looking ahead

The next chapter begins with some very baffling and counterintuitive findings from studies done by relationship researchers, which will lead us into our discussion of the *Idealist* approach to friendship.

Chapter 10

Idealists: My friends would do anything for me

Treat your friends as you do your pictures, and place them in their best light.

–Jennie Jerome Churchill

I should begin by acknowledging that the *Idealist* style of friendship is the least intuitive of the six styles, because it is derived from a series of studies by relationship researchers that, to some, may defy common sense. These studies focus on romantic relationships and I will describe them first before applying their findings to close friendships.

The myopia of falling in love

We've all heard the expression "love is blind." Both research and common experience attest to the truth of this maxim. People falling in love see the object of their desires with rose-colored glasses, filtering out those subtle, and perhaps not-so-subtle, signs of problems that could dampen enthusiasm for their mate, once the initial rush of romance has passed.

For the man in love, "She's bright, charming, caring, a good conversationalist, attractive and furthermore, she's head-over-heels in love with me." For the woman in love, "He's handsome, sensitive, loving, fun to be with, a great conversationalist and furthermore, he's head-over-heels in love with me." The content of these narratives may vary somewhat, but they all contain exaggerated, idealized scripts extoling virtues of their newfound loves.

When we care about the people falling head-over-heals in love, and they've imaginatively inflated the positive characteristics of their new love interest, we often feel a deep-seated need to enlighten them, to shake them out of their love-struck stupor, to help them see their new romance realistically, and avoid being disappointed and hurt when reality finally sets in.

Love is the triumph of imagination over intelligence.

-Henry Louis Mencken

After all, wouldn't it be better to love and accept someone as he or she really is, rather than holding on to some idealized fantasy, preventing one from seeing the authentic person? It is easy to see why such fantasies would be unhealthy, that it would be more adaptive in the long run to see one's love interest realistically, with good and not-so-good features, the beauty spots as well as the warts.

The "wisdom" of relationship researchers

Well, relationship researchers don't agree. In fact, they've collected lots of data suggesting just the opposite is true, that idealizing one's romantic partner actually leads to a healthier relationship, in both the short and long term. When dating couples are tested, those who idealize their partners, or as relationship researchers put it, "hold positive illusions" about them, are more likely to be deeper in love, have less conflict, and still be in the relationship a year later.

Before going on, it may be worth mentioning how they measure such things: Couples are asked to rate themselves and their spouses on a number of traits or characteristics, from "lovingness" all the way down to "punctuality." Then, they compare A's ratings of B to B's ratings of him or her self. If A's ratings of B are much more positive than B's self-ratings, A can be said to hold positive illusions about B. So if I rate my wife on "lovingness" and other traits higher than she would rate herself, I can be said to hold positive illusions about her.

Among married couples, those holding positive illusions about their mates were happier in their relationships, had less conflict, and felt closer to one another. At least one study shows that idealizing couples are less likely to divorce years later. Apparently, seeing one's mate with rose-colored glasses actually enhances the relationship and is therefore healthy and adaptive for partners in love, at least in USAer culture.

Love is a great beautifier.

–Louisa May Alcott

What is even more fascinating (and a bit off topic, but I can't resist), in longitudinal studies of these phenomena, relationship researchers have found that the positive illusions we hold for our mates may become self-fulfilling over time. If I rate my spouse higher on punctuality than she rates herself, two years later, completing the same ratings, we would both agree that she is highly punctual. Sandra Murray and her colleagues entitled one such research report, "Love is not blind, but prescient." Apparently, more often than not, we become the person our mates idealize us to be.

I am sure many of you are rolling your eyes or scratching your heads at these findings. But the robustness of the data renders this research quite convincing.

Is love delusion?

Subsequent research has clarified and limited this principle only a little bit. Holding these positive illusions about one's mate is not equivalent to being delusional—one does see the other's faults. It seems to be more a matter of "spin," an inclination to see those faults within the idealized relationship as a whole, where the positive qualities overshadow or compensate for the faults.

It is also important to note these studies form just a small part of a very large body of research about the factors that make marriages work. John Gottman and other scholars have done comprehensive and convincing research in this field and there is one theme that runs throughout all of this work: The key to a happy marriage is hanging on to a fundamental optimism that things will work out between you and your mate in the long run. Thus, the positive illusions I'm referring to here are just one more example of the importance of maintaining an optimistic outlook in a marriage.

In other cultures?

Does idealizing one's mate result in longer, happier marriages in other cultures as well? Japanese researchers have tried to replicate these findings in their country, for example, and found that spouses do hold positive illusions about each other. But it is too early to tell if these positive illusions are associated with longer, happier marriages.

Furthermore, they have discovered a fundamental problem with a basic element of this research. Recall that positive illusions are inferred when A's ratings of B are greater than B's self-ratings. When these studies are done in the U.S., self-ratings are typically quite high—USAers rate themselves as "above average" on nearly everything. So positive illusions are inferred when your mate rates you even higher than your already inflated self-ratings. Personal pride, or maintaining a healthy self-esteem, is a cultural norm in the U.S., and the positive self-ratings stem from that value.

In Japan, the opposite is true; nearly everyone rates him or herself as below average on nearly everything. Personal modesty is a cultural value in Japan. So given the low baseline, it is much easier for your spouse's ratings to surpass your own, thus implying idealization. But that leaves open the question whether this is idealization or simply a side effect of exaggerated modesty at work. Regardless, the research can't be considered equivalent in Japan.

Friends versus lovers

I'd like to bring the discussion back to friendship and start with a comparison between these two kinds of close relationships, romance and friendship. According to relationship researchers, when compared to friendships, romantic relationships tend to be more intimate, passionate, committed, exclusive, and possessive. And of course, romantic relationships carry a sexual dimension that is absent from the way relationship researchers think of friendship.

Complicating this comparison, however, is the fact that many married people think of their spouse as their "best friend." Furthermore, most romantic relationships start out as friendships and some people, at least, are able to maintain friendly relations with their past romantic partners. And then there are the so-called "friends with benefits," which refers to sexual relationships that are explicitly labeled as non-romantic and not emotionally committed. So the lines of distinction between romantic relationships and friendships are never clear-cut.

Nearly everyone agrees they have many psychological aspects in common. Both provide a similar set of benefits: Warmth, acceptance, support, fun, companionship, and so forth. Many of the theories developed by relationship researchers apply equally to both.

Idealizing our friends?

Given all these similarities, the question becomes, do close friends tend to idealize each other as romantic couples do? There are lots of reasons to argue they do, especially in the U.S. In my questionnaire research, USAers generally rated their closest friends as having more positive traits than did respondents in other cultures.

I use these findings and other arguments to follow as the basis for the *Idealist* style of friendship. *Idealists* tend to see their friends in the most glowing of terms, rating them as intelligent, charming, interesting, and willing "to do anything for me." Other researchers report findings that at least hint at the possibility that idealistic thinking influences USAer friendships. For example, Dorothy Flannagan and her colleagues at the University of Texas found that people tend to bias their evaluations of friends in positive ways in order to enhance these relationships. Sharad Goel and colleagues at Yahoo! Research found that Facebook users often overestimate the similarity of attitudes and opinions of their friends. A tendency to idealize our friends provides a potential explanation for these findings.

The deepest principle in human nature is the craving to be appreciated.

–William James

Still other research suggests that, as is the case in romantic relationships, rating our friends very positively can serve a self-enhancement function. If I rate my friend as intelligent and that he would do almost anything for me, I am indirectly saying I am intelligent as well and I merit having a friend who would do almost anything for me. As I've mentioned several times now, in the U.S., there is a lot of social pressure to maintain positive self-esteem, and our friends, or at least our perceptions of them, play an important role in boosting our egos. This is less likely to be the case in Japan or Korea for example, where the need for group belongingness trumps the need for self-enhancement.

To summarize all of this research talk so far, given the initial data that USAers hold positive illusions about those who are dear to them, and given the constant need in this highly individualistic culture to maintain one's own self-esteem, one can interpret the exceptionally positive ratings of USAers about their friends as indicating an inclination toward idealizing these relationships.

A long history of idealizing our friends

I should hasten to add that idealizing friendships is not a novel concept; it has a very long history in Western thought. Joseph Epstein has written a very perceptive memoire entitled *Friendship: An Exposé* where he outlines this historical trend among philosophers and writers down through the ages. Aristotle argued true friendship can only occur between men of virtue, and their mutual attraction grows out of the goodness they see in each other. A few centuries later, Cicero thought good friends must agree on everything, basking in the warmth and affection of their common beliefs. Phew! One can't get much more idealistic than that!

Epstein goes on to write about the most famous case of idealized friendship in all of recorded history as that between Michel de Montaigne and Étienne de la Boétie in the 16th century. Montaigne wrote extensively about their friendship, rhapsodizing it as "perfect, inviolate, and entire." But he wrote this many years after his friend's death, and in all of his descriptions, Epstein points out quite revealingly, Montaigne never once refers to a specific incident or anecdote regarding their time together. He waxes long and poetic about their friendship, mostly about its abstract qualities, as "temperate," "equal," "constant," and "gentle," but never once touches down to the real world, to the give and take of everyday friendships.

Epstein bluntly asserts that real life friendships aren't like that. A theme running throughout his book cautions against the natural tendency to idealize these relationships. The assumption that this tendency exists is never questioned. Current-day communication scholars such as William Rawlins have written for decades about the tensions between our tendencies to idealize our friendships and the realities of these relationships as they play out in our day-to-day lives.

My data suggest that the tendency to idealize friendship is much more prevalent in some cultures compared to others.

That can-do spirit

In the U.S., idealism and optimism are values that also have a long history, and I'll tick off just a few examples. De Tocqueville was the first to note that Americans see themselves and their experiment with democracy as "exceptional." In 1952, Norman Vincent Peale published his highly influential book, "*The Power of Positive Thinking*." One of the most significant movements in psychology today is called Positive Psychology, led primarily by Martin E. P. Seligman, the former president of the American Psychological Association. The fact that USAers have a tendency to idealize their close relationships must be seen in this broader historical context of a culture that has always leaned toward optimism and idealism.

> *Friendship is a strong and habitual inclination in two persons to promote the good and happiness of one another.*
>
> –Eustace Budgell

This tendency is clearly expressed when USAers are asked to rate almost anything about themselves. No matter the issue or the setting, whether it is one's personal attractiveness, expectations about one's future accomplishments, or one's chances of winning the lottery, USAers tend to project a higher degree of optimism about things in their lives than do peoples in most other cultures. So rating our spouse or best friend very highly may be just another example of this more generic positive outlook.

This larger-than-life optimism and idealism does have a downside. Barbara Ehrenreich has written a very poignant, sometimes funny, but always perceptive social history and commentary entitled *Bright-Sided*, in which she critically examines the USAer tendency for unfettered idealization and optimism. She recounts that while undergoing treatment for breast cancer, people around her, including other cancer patients, would rebuke her scornfully for not always maintaining a cheerful, optimistic demeanor. They viewed her anxiety and anger as maladaptive emotional blocks, signaling a clear need for serious therapy.

She argues throughout her book that the constant social demand for positive thinking in the U.S. can be detrimental to honestly facing life's more difficult moments.

Other historians and social commentators have argued that USAer optimism reflects the modern day legacy of the early pioneering spirit, the deep-seated self-reliance that is so uniquely and unchangeably USAer.

What does it mean to be an *Idealist* friend?

So the USAer inclination to idealize their friendships must be seen as just one aspect of a more generalized tendency toward optimism. The *Idealist* style reflects primarily how USAers perceive and think about their closest friendships and as such, it isn't always obvious from their outward behavior. But it does show up in their friendship in various ways that are worth examining more closely.

For example, their idealized perceptions of their friends help to explain why USAers often rate their friendships as closer or more intimate than do respondents of other cultures, even collectivist cultures where friends presumably depend on each other more in their everyday lives. If we give very positive ratings to a question like, "I would do almost anything for my friend," we may be saying more about how we think about this friend rather than things we've actually done for this friend in the past.

Like the *Independent* style of friendship discussed in Chapter Five, close *Idealist* friends tend to be each other's greatest fans, constantly there for each other, to help their friends through difficult times, not by intervening in their lives, but by words of encouragement which serve to boost their egos. Such ego boosting provides much appreciated comfort in dealing with life's challenges.

A man should keep his friendships in constant repair.

–Samuel Johnson

Good *Idealist* friends are pillars of support for each other, especially ego support, and herein lies the greatest advantage of this style of friendship. You can count on *Idealist* friends to provide a helping hand to your morale.

All of this positivity is part of a strategy to ensure these friendships endure, since they are considered fragile relationships in *Idealist* cultures. They must be constantly maintained if they are to flourish.

Without regular attention, they will simply fade away. Nothing in their friendships can be taken for granted. This helps explain the findings mentioned in the last chapter why *Idealist* friends tend to keep their interactions in an upbeat, positive, reassuring tone.

Idealists rarely criticize a friend directly or even disagree on matters seen as important. To do so would indicate a lack of acceptance. When *Idealists* do disagree on an important issue that can't be avoided, they end up "agreeing to disagree" which is actually a sort of code for deciding not to discuss the issue any longer.

Saving face

Idealists are constantly aware of face issues when they deal with their closest friends. Although the U.S. is not considered a face culture, the concept does apply to their close friendships. They prefer to avoid direct confrontation or disagreements about matters critical to one's self-concept.

Similarly, even though directness in communication is a trait USAers are famous for, especially in business settings, saying what we mean and meaning what we say, they tend to employ very indirect forms of communication when it comes to dealing with difficult issues with their closest friends. They avoid any talk that would disrespect their friend's individuality, saying what the friend wants to hear rather than what might be best for him or her in the long run.

It's important to our friends to believe that we are unreservedly frank with them, and important to the friendship that we are not.

–Mignon McLaughlin

Amy's wisdom

I love to read "Ask Amy," the syndicated advice column by Amy Dickinson that appears in our local newspaper, especially when it concerns a conflict the letter-writer is having with a close friend. In these cases, you can always count on Amy. Her advice is always the same, without exception. She simply advises the letter-writer to tell the friend what he or she needs to know but may not want to hear. Amy will often provide the actual words for the letter-writer to use, but these words are never anything more than communicating clearly and directly to the friend about the problem.

Somehow, telling the friend what he or she needs to hear is considered expert advice, something that wouldn't occur to the letter-writer otherwise. When it comes to their closest friends, USAer *Idealists* tend to represent a genuine face culture, by handling difficult friendship matters very indirectly, with a subtlety and sensitivity that would rival the communication patterns often attributed to Asian cultures. And when that doesn't work, they write and "ask Amy."

Jennifer and Lisa, *Idealist* friends

A hypothetical example may help: Suppose Lisa is telling her close *Idealist* friend Jennifer about problems she is having at work. This topic has come up often and Jennifer has heard many similar stories in the past. It is clear to Jennifer that Lisa does things at work to create much of the tension she is complaining about. For example, she often goes over the head of her boss to get her way about certain matters relevant to her job. She does other things that could be seen as invalidating her boss's existence. In so many ways, Lisa is her own worst enemy at work. Jennifer has come to this conclusion often.

> *There are times that when truth and kindness conflict one ought to choose kindness, especially when a little honesty is better than a lot.*
>
> –Leroy Jack Syrop

However, as *Idealist* friends, Jennifer is very unlikely to confront Lisa directly with her thinking on the matter. Lisa is upset and she sought Jennifer out to "have someone to talk to" about her problems at work. To confront her now with her own mistakes would not be the supportive thing to do. The key point here is that the USAer reticence to criticize a close friend stems from their tendency to idealize their friends and friendships. The role of the *Idealist* friend is to be there for them, to stick up for them, to take their point of view, to help them deal with their problems with words of encouragement.

I must be careful not overstate my case here. Taking the side of a close friend does have limits among USAers, and seems to be confined to situations where the two friends are talking in private about personal matters. As we saw in Chapter Four with the Trompenaars' study, if a USAer is riding in the car of a friend who is speeding and hits a pedestrian, he or she is likely to testify in a court of law that the friend was indeed speeding, rather than say what is needed to help the friend avoid a jail sentence.

Idealists and "jock talk"

Some of you, especially if you are a guy, might not be able to identify with the notion that friends in the U.S. tend to provide only positive, non-critical support. After all, just earlier today, one of my handball buddies, out on the court, in the heat of the game, was telling me,

"What a cute shot, girly boy, where's your tutu?"

And of course, I responded with, "At least I got the point, fatso!"

"Just shut up and serve the ball, Ms. Tutu girly boy," and on and on and on it goes.

Men's sports venues and locker rooms are full of such put-down banter, one constantly trying to outdo the other. How do you square such talk with the idea that USAer friends tend to support each other, boosting egos rather than criticizing? I would argue that such macho talk is done entirely in jest, but more importantly, it is seldom truly critical. There are subtle but important limits to such banter.

Idealist men friends can put each other down in creative and often vulgar ways, they can argue about sports or even politics, but there are unspoken barriers that are never breached. They are unlikely to disparage a friend regarding issues that really matter,

> *The only service a friend can really render is to keep up your courage by holding up to you a mirror in which you can see a noble image of yourself.*
>
> –George Bernard Shaw

such as one's competence at work or one's choice of romantic partner, things that would truly be threatening to one's ego. I don't think such issues are off limits among close *Realist* friends.

Another example of idealization and maintaining face?

There is one version of idealization that did not show up in my limited data sets, but colleagues have mentioned it during the question-and-answer segments of my presentations at conferences for cross-cultural researchers. At a recent conference, for example, a USAer woman who had been living for a number of years in Mexico and was married to a Mexican man, asked why her very close Mexican friends occasionally made promises or committed to doing something and then failed to follow through with it?

She emphasized that these were very close friends, like family members, and yet they would, on occasion, promise to do something for her that was rather important or significant, like attending her son's graduation ceremony, and then they didn't show up. A few interculturalists from Central and South America have mentioned that this kind of thing happens among friends in some of their cultures as well. In some respects, it fits the idealization patterns I describe in this chapter.

One could see this pattern of broken promises as an attempt to maintain face with a friend. These promises are made when the friends are face to face, where doing or saying things that enhance the relationship serve to promote warm feelings for each other. The promise-makers may be thinking idealistically rather than realistically about what they can do for the friend. They get carried away with strong feelings of the moment, feelings that cause them to want to please an important friend, with the result of promising more than they can reasonably deliver.

Consistent with the *Idealist* style, the self-esteem or the egos of the friends might also play a role. Making exaggerated commitments may enhance one's own ego—after all, only a very good friend could make such a promise. Interculturalists who are familiar with this friendship phenomenon tend to agree such commitments are very well intentioned, allowing both friends to feel good at the moment.

As in other issues of face, the commitments are not honored some time in the future, when the friends are no longer face-to-face. For whatever reason, a scheduling conflict, an emergency, or other circumstances conspire to prevent one from following through with the well-intentioned commitment.

One flaw in this interpretation is the fact that Central and South American countries are generally considered collectivist cultures, and my concept of *Idealist* friendships is associated more with individualist cultures. Perhaps this is one more example where the individualist-collectivist dimension carries implications that are not very consistent when applied to friendships.

Idealists:

*Tend to hold positive illusions about their closest friends

*Think about their friends as having mostly positive traits

*On surveys, rate their friends higher than do *Realists*

*Rate friends positively in order to enhance their own self-esteem

*Tend to avoid strong disagreement with close friends

*Emphasize the positive when in the company of their friends

*Are concerned about issues of face with their closest friends

*Their positive ratings result in higher scores on closeness

*See friendships as fragile, needing constant "maintenance"

An *Idealist* and a *Realist* as friends

So what happens when an *Idealist* and a *Realist* try to forge a friendship with each other? Most typically, it is the blunt talk of the *Realist* that creates problems for this friendship combination. The *Idealist* tends to interpret strong disagreement about any issue as personal rejection and a lack of the validation they are accustomed to receiving from close friends.

In my work with international students, many of whom were much more *Realist* in their friendship orientations, I saw this issue as a primary stumbling block in their friendships with the more *Idealist* USAers. Sometimes they would strongly disagree with a USAer student, and it could be about anything, including sensitive issues such as politics, or one's basic philosophy of life. Or it could concern much less controversial issues like music, sports or clothes. *Idealist* USAers tended to see their disagreeing as arrogance, or a put-down, an indication that the *Realist* international students didn't like them and wasn't interested in friendship.

Realists, on the other hand, have a problem with the *Idealists'* inclination to constantly speak in a positive, supportive way, trying to

> *Whenever you're in conflict with someone, there is one factor that can make the difference between damaging your relationship and deepening it. That factor is attitude.*
>
> –Timothy Bentley

boost their egos. It comes off as shallow and insincere, or as inappropriate flattery. It just doesn't feel like true friendship. In addition, the *Idealist* seeks to have his or her own ego stroked by the friend, which is perceived as self-centered and egotistical by the *Realist*.

The *Realist* may long for conversations that dig deep into important issues, which can be fun and help cement the feeling of having a very good friend to share such ideas with, even when there is strong disagreement. To the *Realist*, the *Idealist* seems nice and friendly, but lacking in substance and commitment. A Thai student at my university expressed this perspective most succinctly, saying, "I often wonder who is really behind that smiling face."

Clearly, for the *Idealists* and *Realists* to form a mutually satisfying friendship, there needs to be some open-mindedness on how they see the role of the supportive friend.

As always, I would like to caution about these cultural stereotypes. My assertion that USAers tend to be *Idealists* who rarely directly criticize their friends on important issues is a gross generalization, with frequent exceptions. As with all cultural norms, there are important regional differences. Inner city New Yorkers can be much more direct with both compliments and criticism than are people in the southeast where I live. Stereotypically, southerners are masters of the indirect put-down, bless their hearts!

Looking ahead

The next chapter looks at the multiple benefits of cultivating close and satisfying friendships. I offer it to motivate you to take your friendships seriously, invest in them, cherish them and at the same time, reap the rewards of having people around who genuinely care.

Chapter 11

Friends can be good medicine

One loyal friend is worth ten thousand relatives.

–Euripides

Imagine an older guy, we'll call him Ralph, someone in his 60's. Actually he's not such an old guy now that I think about it, but an unfortunate fellow nonetheless since he just had a heart attack, and now finds himself in the hospital. After major surgery and a stint in the intensive care unit, Ralph's condition has stabilized. He's now out of danger, but he'll have a long recovery ahead of him.

Ralph expects to spend a couple more days in the hospital before returning home for a long regimen of prescribed exercise and rehabilitation. While in the hospital, he gets visitors, some of them family members, but also a number of friends stop by to chat and provide some much needed encouragement. The visits from friends, as it turns out, appear to be critical to his recovery as well as reducing his chances of a recurrence down the road. Had Ralph not had these visitors, or had his visitors been only family members, his chances of a full recovery would be greatly diminished.

Friends can be good medicine and there is a plethora of data to support this contention. This chapter aims to describe those findings and explain all of the far-reaching benefits that result from spending quality time with good friends.

Are USAers losing out?

A growing body of research suggests that USAers in particular may be undervaluing their friendships, so I'm aiming this chapter directly at them, and to people of other cultures who've begun to lose contact with their closest friends.

I have argued throughout this book that USAers are capable of close and fulfilling friendships, despite their international reputation to the contrary. Their *Independent* and *Includer* versions of friendship simply appear rather shallow and insincere to others, but that renders them no less meaningful or impactful in their lives. This chapter documents that spending time with good friends, as the vast majority of USAers claim to do, is associated with significant health benefits. It's worth noting that most of these studies were conducted in the U.S.

Some people go to priests; others to poetry; I to my friends.

-Virginia Woolf

These data would make no sense at all if USAer friendships were characteristically shallow and insignificant.

Yet, there are some controversial studies showing that over the last decade or so, the average USAer's circle of close friends—ones they can confide in—has grown smaller and smaller. For example, one study showed that the number of people saying they had no one in their lives with whom they could discuss personal matters has nearly tripled in the last twenty years. Most argue this sad state of affairs is the result of our ever-expanding number of hours devoted to work per week.

But these studies are controversial because of some methodological issues, and also because some of them ignore the widespread usage of social media such as Facebook, which is changing the way people stay in contact. Still, it may be true that USAers are spending less actual face time with friends, and in this sense they may be experiencing a loss of connectedness.

In my own studies that looked at friendships among USAers of all ages, where respondents were required to focus their responses on a specific close friend, I was always surprised by the number of them, mostly middle-aged men, who would say they had no one in that category. That is, they had no one they thought of as a close friend they could use as the focus of their responses on my questionnaire. As I replicated these studies over the years, while still a small minority, their numbers seemed to be increasing.

An overview

Despite intending this chapter for USAers, the principles I describe apply to everyone, no matter the cultural background. These studies provide a fascinating picture of the benefits, especially the health benefits, both physical and psychological of spending time with close friends.

In perusing this literature, I discovered much of the research tends to focus on three groups. The first consists of people who are experiencing a health crisis, for example, women with breast cancer or men with cardiovascular disease. There is a lot of research showing that people in these difficult circumstances who have supportive friends in addition to supportive family members fare remarkably better.

When you face a crisis, you know who your true friends are.

–Earvin "Magic" Johnson

The other two groups are adolescents and older adults, two time periods in everyone's life when having close friends is critically important. For adolescents, having good friends helps smooth the transition from depending on parents and other family members to making one's own way out into the adult world. These studies show that having healthy, fulfilling friendships is associated with less drug use, avoiding risky sexual behavior, lower levels of anxiety and depression, and a healthier personality, in addition to a number of other benefits that would apply to individuals of all ages.

Growing older

Of special interest to me are the studies focused on older adults since they are quite revealing of the special role friends play in our lives. I will discuss them in some detail, and then turn to research that would apply to people of all ages.

As we grow older, the need for assistance gradually increases for many of us. Health issues arise and accumulate, mobility becomes challenging, and the deaths of friends and partners begin to take a toll. Researchers in the field of gerontology are very sensitive to factors that impact one's quality of life in later years, and close, satisfying friendships have been shown to be among the most critical ones. Older adults are healthier and happier, and they live longer when they make time for their close friends.

Living longer

Let's look first at the effects on longevity, which can be quite dramatic. Two recent books have gained a lot of public attention in this area: Christakis and Fowler's book entitled *Connected*, which is about the power of social networks to impact every aspect of our daily lives, and Friedman and Martin's examination of factors influencing longevity, entitled *The Longevity Project*. Both show that the number of people in one's social network seems to be the critical factor in living to a ripe old age and enjoying the trip getting there. Simply having more friends, colleagues, and associates as well as family members in one's network—being widely connected—is strongly associated with longevity.

When I'm in front of an audience, all that love and vitality sweeps over me and I forget my age.

–George Burns

A recent overview by Julianne Holt-Lunstad and colleagues of 140 studies that examined the longevity of over 300,000 individuals also demonstrated that being well connected was associated, on average, with a 50% higher chance of survival over the time periods of the individual studies. One limitation, like many studies in the field, is that it didn't distinguish between the effects of family ties and friendship ties. It is clear, however, both connections are important.

If I'd known I was gonna live this long, I'd have taken better care of myself.

–Eubie Blake

Individual studies that do make this distinction have produced astounding effects demonstrating the importance of friendships. An Australian study, for example, by Lynne Giles and colleagues showed that friends were far more important to longevity than family ties. Berkman and Syme found in their longitudinal study of 7,000 people in California that those who claimed to be friendless were twice as likely to die during the 9-year period of the study compared to those who were more connected.

Most of these findings are quite robust. In terms of their correlations, not having satisfying friendships and other close relationships is as detrimental to one's longevity as smoking a pack of cigarettes a day or being obese and sedentary.

Good friends versus being friendly

So which is more important, being well connected with a large network of friends and acquaintances, or having a small group of very close friends one can count on? I could talk long about this controversy in the research, since there are different groups, citing different studies, who argue for each side of this debate. My take on this issue is that both are important. When it comes to one's closest friends, the quality of these relationships is the critical issue regarding health benefits. When it comes to other friends, people in one's social network who are friends, but not considered "close friends," it is sheer numbers that matter.

Friendship is a sheltering tree.

–Samuel Taylor Coleridge

One recent large-scale cross-cultural study by Jaap Denissen and colleagues validates this distinction directly. Apparently, having a few very satisfying friendships works just as well as having a large number of genial, if less committed, social connections.

Friendly advice versus boosting our morale

Moving on from the longevity research, let's now look more directly at the health benefits of close friendship for the elderly. To me, the most interesting studies are those that pit the beneficial effects of family relationships in direct contrast to friendships, allowing the researchers to parcel out the distinct advantages of each. Let's go back to Ralph, who introduced this chapter. Recall that he is the older gentleman facing a long recovery after a severe heart attack.

Lots of studies show the distinctive advantage of having satisfying friendships for scenarios like this one. I've tried to ferret out exactly why time spent with friends is so strongly related to a healthier prognosis. Do Ralph's friends encourage him to lose weight, get more exercise, and eat more fruits and vegetables? Is that the critical factor? This is the hypothesis favored by sociologists: Friends lead to behavioral changes resulting in a healthier lifestyle. Christakis and Fowler's book on network effects show quite convincingly that factors such as obesity are strongly influenced by the people around us, even by friends of our friends, and friends of their friends.

While these data show very clear effects, overall, I don't find these studies very convincing. One's friends, in the U.S. at least, seldom offer this kind of advice, and when they do, one rarely abides by it. The contagion effects of the network studies don't seem to apply to Ralph's case, and furthermore, these effects appear to have little to do with friends offering advice. Looking at cardiovascular disease specifically, the positive influence of friends on one's prognosis seems to follow a different psychological path.

Among those whom I like or admire, I can find no common denominator, but among those whom I love, I can: all of them make me laugh.

–W.H. Auden

Spending time with friends tends to boost our self-esteem, we feel better about ourselves, and it is our enhanced self-esteem that lowers anxiety and depression, which apparently have very direct effects on cardiac functioning. This morale boost also leaves us with more courage to face these health challenges. Hospital visits from family members do not produce comparable increases in self-esteem.

Many sides of self-esteem

As an aside, I think it important to clarify how psychologists use this term self-esteem. A very large number of studies show that low self-esteem is a potent risk factor for many aspects of physical and mental health. So it is critical to understand the various applications of this concept. Self-esteem is much more than just one's ego, although certainly, that's part of it.

Friendship improves happiness, and abates misery, by doubling our joys, and dividing our grief.

–Marcus Tullius Cicero

In some contexts, psychological researchers use the term self-esteem to refer to one's frame of mind at a given point in time, somewhat like one's mood. How would you describe your mood at this very moment, good or bad, optimistic or pessimistic, confident or discouraged? In this case, they are referring to a very transient feeling, one that fluctuates throughout the day, coinciding with one's minor experiences of success or failure, enjoyment or frustration.

Another version of self-esteem applies the concept to specific tasks—how confident do you feel that you can do a particular task well? This version of self-esteem is also transient depending completely on the nature of the task, such as doing math problems in your head, and your feelings of competence with respect to that task. Psychologists also view self-esteem as a personality characteristic, which some people have more of than others. They have lots of different ways of measuring this stable trait. Lastly, cultures have been compared on their level of self-esteem, with some cultures valuing this personal characteristic more than others.

Friends as health agents

In the case of Ralph and his recovery from a heart attack, the distinct advantage of spending time with friends involves a boost to his self-esteem, leaving him in a more positive frame of mind. The greatest impact of close friends, thus, is in the realm of one's morale and emotions. Men tend not to think of their friendships in these terms, but the truth is, friends quite often make us feel better. They make us happy.

Although evidence still isn't clear on this, I suspect that the positive impact of close friends is most evident in face-to-face encounters compared to more indirect means of connecting such as through Facebook, Twitter, or email. And spending time with friends is beneficial for the functioning of the heart. For the elderly, family members simply don't produce the same effects.

We laugh a lot. That's for sure. Sure beats the alternative, doesn't it?

–Betty White

This is not to say that family relationships don't play an important supportive role in the realm of elder care. Research suggests that support from family members (including a spouse) doesn't have much of an effect on self-esteem and other similar measures. However, its absence is devastating on all measures of wellbeing.

Family members provide a kind of baseline support without which the elderly face a very challenging life. Having great friendships rarely compensates for a lack of family in this respect. However, in situations where the family support is at least adequate or better, it is their friendships that provide a zest for life, a boost to self-esteem, and a sense of optimism about the present and the future.

An example close to home

Nine years ago, my wife Susan's mother Phyllis moved from the Boston area to a home near ours in Charlotte in order to be near family when the time arrived for her to need greater care.

From the time I first met Phyllis, there was one thing about her I've admired greatly, and that is the value she places on her closest friendships. Phyllis knows more about the ins and outs, the practicalities of making good friends and keeping them, compared to any relationship researcher in the business. Even these many years later, she stays in weekly contact with her closest friends in Boston, in addition to making very devoted new friends here in Charlotte whom she sees several times a week. Many of her Boston friends made the trip down here last year to help her celebrate her 90th birthday.

Friends are the sunshine of life.

–John Hay

Phyllis exemplifies in so many ways the points I am trying to make about the elderly and the role of friendships in their lives. To be clear, Phyllis loves to spend time with her two daughters and she'll go through great pains to make that happen. But this time spent with family doesn't produce a clear or reliable enhancement of her morale. She doesn't always project the image of a happy camper at family gatherings. But whenever she spends time with friends, which is as often as she possibly can, she is nearly always in a terrific mood.

The fall that wasn't

Even anticipating spending time with friends puts a spring in her step. Once, a couple of years ago, she took a misstep and fell flat on her face. Falls both before and after this particular incident have been devastating—a broken pelvis, several cracked vertebrae, as well as long stays in the hospital and rehabilitation clinics.

But this fall occurred at a social gathering that included close friends, and she was anticipating flying to Boston just a week later to visit her long-time friends. She popped right back up, shook off any attempts to help her, and kept right on chattering away with her friends as if nothing at all had happened. Both Susan and I witnessed the event in total disbelief. We were certain we would be spending another sleepless night in the emergency room.

The greatest healing therapy is friendship and love.

–Hubert Humphrey

I am not trying to argue that friends can cushion falls and prevent fractures—there is no evidence at all to support such a contention. What I am arguing is that friends in old age have a very powerful effect on one's morale, providing an awesome drive to shake off minor aches and pains, to go on enjoying the truly important moments in one's life.

The role of friends versus families

For Phyllis, like many older adults, friends provide continuity in her life. They remind her of the person she was before she had children, who she became while she was raising them, and how things changed after they left the nest. They share this history and validate her perspective on life.

The only thing to do is to hug one's friends tight and do one's job.

–Edith Wharton

They reinforce her qualities as a unique individual, her admirable qualities, those traits that attracted them to her as a friend in the first place. Friendships are voluntary relationships, and to her friends, she is an interesting, lovable, valuable human being, someone they actively choose to spend time with. They see her as so much more than a mother or a grandmother. And the fact that she returns all of these sentiments to them allows her to feel useful and socially competent, as an equal partner in their relationships.

In recent years, as she has begun to require more care giving from Susan and me, it has been much more difficult for her to feel like an equal partner in our relationships as a family. This fact alone means that spending time with us doesn't produce the same kind of boost to her morale she gets from friends.

There is a tendency for our time together to feel more and more routine. We always invite her over for dinner on Sunday evenings. While we all typically enjoy this time together, it can sometimes feel a bit mundane. Much of our conversation revolves around practical matters—

scheduling doctors' visits, taking care of bills, organizing her transportation needs.

Phyllis was a single mother who was fiercely independent and self-sufficient her entire life. Finding herself depending on us has been very difficult for her. But she knows she can count on us to take care of her when the need arises. She has had four major medical emergencies over the past nine years and she credits us for pulling her through them. To a large extent, her feelings of wellbeing stem from the sense of security we provide. She is very grateful we are always there for her, and she expresses her feelings about these matters often and with deep sincerity. We play a critical role in her everyday sense of wellbeing.

There is nothing better than the encouragement of a good friend.

-Katherine Hathaway

But with her friends, things are simply much more enjoyable; it's all about companionship and having fun together. And that counts for a great deal. We provide some security; her friends give her gusto for living!

An adolescent example

Here is another way of expressing the contrast between the roles of family members versus friends in helping someone facing a health crisis. Relationship researchers distinguish between instrumental support, which typically refers to the concrete assistance provided by family members versus the emotional support oftentimes provided more effectively by friends.

Annette LaGreca and colleagues provide an insightful example of an adolescent boy who just learned he has diabetes. The news was devastating, affecting every aspect of his day-to-day life. As he struggled to find some equilibrium, it was clear family members were there to provide the needed instrumental support, helping with issues like insulin injections, glucose monitoring, and nutrition.

His friends played almost no role on that front. But where their presence seemed to have the greatest impact was to boost his morale, to help him find the courage to put this disease into a broader perspective in his everyday life. The truth is we need both.

What about the rest of us?

Let's turn now to the research that would apply to friends of every age and the influence they have on our health and wellbeing. In a nutshell, these studies show very convincingly that spending quality time with friends influences our bodies in measureable ways by improving the functioning of the cardiovascular system, the nervous system, the endocrine (hormonal) system as well as the immune system. The benefits of friends on one's wellbeing are especially evident after stressful events.

In laboratory studies, researchers can show how such events strain the cardiovascular system, for example. These measureable reactions of the heart and circulatory system have been clearly associated with cardiovascular diseases. A major part of rehabilitation for cardiac patients involves reducing stressors in their lives since these have been shown to directly influence cardiac functioning in ways that contribute to the disease.

Just being there or not

These studies have shown repeatedly that the heart will demonstrate much more attenuated reactions to stress when there is a friend present. In some studies, the friend is conversing with the experimental participant, providing some encouraging words, or simply distracting the participant from the stressful annoyances being applied by the researcher. (I should note that people who volunteer for these studies are told very clearly in advance the nature of the stressors they will be experiencing. All researchers today follow very strict ethical guidelines.)

Friendship ... is firm ground in a bog.

–Stella Maria Sarah Miles Franklin

In other studies, the friend is merely present, and they are not interacting. Yet the results are quite similar. Simply having a friend with you reduces harmful cardiac reactions to stress.

As important as these findings are, you might be saying there's nothing surprising here. You may be quite aware of the calming effect being with a good friend can produce. But in the real world—fighting traffic on the way to work, dealing with all of the stressors on the job, and perhaps facing even more conflict upon returning home—you can't take your friends with you all day just to dampen the negative physiological effects of all these day-to-day stressors.

Many studies show it really doesn't matter. Spending regular, quality time with friends has very beneficial effects on the cardiovascular system even when the friends are not present at any given moment.

How it works

Let's say that Laura has an anxiety-provoking conflict with her boss at work this morning. This stressor will produce very maladaptive cardiovascular reactions—we needn't go into detail about the physiological nature of these reactions but they can be measured in a variety of ways, implying that many aspects of the circulatory system are being affected.

Laughter is the closest distance between two people.

-Victor Borge

I should point out Laura's physiological reactions would be roughly equivalent whether or not she is someone who values her close friendships. The bigger difference between those who spend regular time with close friends and those who don't comes afterwards.

Let's assume Laura does have a few close friends and she calls one of them to meet for lunch. Together, they commiserate about Laura's unreasonable boss and the awful experience she had earlier in the day. Laura "unloads" much of her negative feelings about the incident and before long both of them are laughing about the matter, perhaps even doing mocking imitations of the overbearing boss.

The trailing, accumulating effects of stress

The critical issue here is not the physiological reactions to the stressful event itself, but rather the lingering effects that tend to follow such events. Some have argued these are far more damaging than the stress reactions of the event itself. Had Laura been someone who makes very little time for her friends, she may have been bothered by the incident the rest of the day, even taking it home with her in the evening, ruminating about what a jerk her boss is, what she wishes she had said during the conflict, thinking about ways to avenge the wrong she had experienced.

These cognitive ruminations and the negative physiological reactions actually feed off each other, especially when anger is involved. Anxious or aggressive thinking produces heightened physiological arousal and this physical agitation encourages even more anxious and aggressive thoughts. It is a vicious circle that is difficult for many people to break out of.

Friendship is certainly the finest balm for the pangs of disappointed love.

-Jane Austen

Having good friends, being well-connected with satisfying relationships, including family and marital relationships, getting along with one's work colleagues and neighbors, affiliating with groups such as churches and community organizations— all of this goes a long way to attenuating the effects of stress on one's physiology. Friends don't have to be present at the time of stress. A few studies have shown that simply knowing they are available, even just thinking about spending time with them, can lower the detrimental effects of stress on the body.

Good friends or just being friendly

It would be good at this point to bring up a controversy that often colors the interpretation of these data. Some have contended that the key underlying factors of good health are actually personality characteristics such as high self-esteem or extraversion. It is not, they argue, that socializing leads to higher self-esteem and its coinciding health benefits, but rather, that extraverts with high self-esteem feel comfortable socializing with others, thus cultivating meaningful and satisfying relationships.

Wear a smile and have friends; wear a scowl and have wrinkles. What do we live for if not to make the world less difficult for each other?

-George Eliot

So the argument goes that some people are just more sociable than others. Their superior health stems more from their outgoing personalities than from the company they keep. There are studies showing that extraverts, especially those with higher self-esteem, tend to handle stress better and have a greater sense of wellbeing. The strong, positive effects of network size, the mere number of friends one can call on, also support this conclusion.

But there are also convincing data showing that personality factors are not the critical issues—spending time with friends is. And one does not have to be an extravert or popular to spend time with friends. The quality of these close friendships does matter. For example, intervention studies show that enhancing one's closest friendships can have positive health effects.

More importantly, large-scale studies that employ clever statistical techniques point to the conclusion that socializing leads to higher self-esteem, not the other way around. Having good friendships and satisfying relationships in general is associated with health benefits, and self-esteem is merely the mediating variable in these findings. Similarly, these studies as well as those focused on the elderly show that it is not so much the case that healthy people are able to attract more friends. Rather, spending time with good friends is associated with being healthier.

Looking at other physiological systems

Sheldon Cohen, and his colleagues at Carnegie Melon University, did a study where they actually infected healthy individuals with common cold viruses to see who would succumb and who wouldn't. They wanted to see how this might be related to their social relationships. (Studies like these always make me wonder about who volunteers for these things!) They found that people with the greatest diversity in their social networks were the least likely to get sick. In other words, having supportive family, neighbors, work mates, as well as good friendships was associated with being more resistant.

The best friend is the man who in wishing me well wishes it for my sake.

–Aristotle

Similar findings and inferences could be presented regarding the endocrine system (e.g. the role of oxytocin in close relationships), and the nervous system (various neurotransmitter substances such as endorphins). But by now, I think you have the picture—cultivating close friendships have very beneficial effects on one's health and wellbeing.

The downside of friendships

If you've been scrutinizing my arguments carefully, you may have noticed that all of this talk about the health benefits of friendships has typically included certain modifiers, such as "good," or "satisfying," or "close" relationships. These qualifiers are important.

The research shows very clearly the reverse is also true, that having ambivalent or conflicted friendships has a decidedly negative impact on one's health and wellbeing. The negative impact of conflicted friendships is especially potent during adolescence, often acting as a stressor and producing elevated mental health symptoms.

Bert Uchino of the University of Utah has been conducting key research on what he refers to as ambivalent relationships. These would include one's friendships that have both highly positive and negative aspects, i.e., things that make the friendship both attractive and bothersome at the same time.

Let's say, for example, I have a close friend with whom I enjoy spending time, going out to hear live music in clubs, playing handball, or just sitting and chatting over lunch. These would be the positive aspects of our friendship. Let's also say he suffers from depression and conversations with him can sometimes become morbid or even hostile. These would be the negative aspects. According to Dr. Uchino, negative aspects of a relationship coexist along with positive elements, and if this ambivalence is strongly felt, the relationship will often result in negative health outcomes.

So the health benefits I have been vaunting for having friends assumes these relationships are close and satisfying, and at the same time, have few significant negatives. Nearly all of these studies measure the quality of these close relationships, and it is these indices of relationship satisfaction that are associated with the health benefits I am describing.

Similarly, having conflict with a friend, in an otherwise harmonious relationship, can be particularly harmful to one's health and wellbeing. Clearly, the support one feels from close friends can be beneficial in putting stressful events in perspective, improving one's sense of confidence, and the health advantages that result. On the other hand, conflict can serve to raise one's anxiety, leading to increased susceptibility to health problems. Such conflict also interferes with a sense of trust that is so critical in the overall functioning of the relationship.

These findings point to the value of keeping our friendships in good, robust health as well. On the positive side, real, impactful conflict in friendships occurs less frequently than it does in marital or family relationships. Regular quality time with friends helps smooth over conflicts and keeps any ambivalent aspects within the broader perspective of a caring friendship.

And as I've noted in Chapters Five and Ten, there is a strong, cultural expectation among USAers to emphasize the positive in their interactions with close friends, which in turn, reduces feelings of ambivalence in their close friendships.

The politics of promoting friendships

I will close this chapter with a story that took place thirty years ago in California. Jerry Brown was governor, the first time, and at that point in our history people were still optimistic that government could play a positive role in citizens' personal lives.

If you lived there at that time, you couldn't help but notice a slogan that was inundating all forms of media, on billboards, TV, radio; on talk shows and in the newspapers; and in community workshops and training sessions that took place in schools, hospitals and churches. Everyone was talking about it. The slogan, "Friends can be good medicine" was a multimillion dollar ad campaign sponsored by the mental health authorities of the state.

Citing earlier versions of the studies that form the bases of this chapter, they thought that by promoting friendships, by making people more aware and encouraging them to spend time with their friends, the state could save on costs associated with public health care. The campaign got a lot of attention, and follow-up research showed that many people actually made an effort to spend more quality time with their friends. Whether this actually impacted the health care costs of the state could not be measured—it is hard to come up with an appropriate comparison or control condition to allow for such inferences.

Today, it seems remarkable to imagine a time when people saw the connection between spending quality time with friends and all of the benefits that can accrue from these relationships.

In this chapter, I have focused primarily on the health outcomes. Of course, there are many, many more significant, if less tangible or measurable benefits of cultivating these important relationships. And I've only talked about being on the receiving end—there are studies that explore the manifold personal rewards and benefits of being a good friend, of being on the providing side of this equation. There's at least one study showing that it truly is much better to give than to receive.

So I encourage you to put this book down this instant, pick up the phone, call a friend, and arrange to meet for coffee or a cocktail. You'll be much better off for it!

Looking ahead

Which do you prefer, men or women as close friends? What do you see as the major difference between men friends and women friends? Are men really from Mars and women from Venus when it comes to how each view their closest friends? These are the questions I will be addressing in the next chapter.

Chapter 12

Mars, Venus and Planet Earth

I don't think any woman in power really has a happy life unless she's got a large number of women friends...because you sometimes must go and sit down and let down your hair with someone you can trust totally.

–Margaret Thatcher

In 1992, John Gray declared men are from Mars and women are from Venus and sold millions of books in the process. He argued men and women are fundamentally quite different in their approaches to close relationships, somewhat akin to coming from radically different cultures.

John Gray himself was not an established relationship researcher and his ideas weren't given much credence by others in the field. Most thought he slanted and exaggerated their findings. Yet, in his defense, he has provided men and women with a vocabulary and a disarming way to talk about their relationships. In my mind, that can't be all bad.

Stereotypes versus reality

But this leaves open the question of how men and women differ in their approaches to close friendships. How do you think about such things? Whom do you think makes for better friends, men or women?

How would you explain your choice? What do you see as key differences between the friendship ways of men and women?

A colleague and I asked these questions of hundreds of volunteers, and we found a sizable minority prefers friendships with the opposite sex. I'll describe some implications of these findings toward the end of this chapter.

A traditional portrayal of gender and friendship holds that men are buddies or companions, doing things together, playing sports or watching it on TV, having fun, valuing loyalty, but often competing with one another. According to these traditional stereotypes, women are supposed to be more oriented to conversation with their friends, often talking about each other and their relationships. Women are seen as more emotional, but also more supportive as friends. The question is, to what extent do these views of friendship still hold today?

Dividers versus Uniters

In the more dispassionate, science-oriented world of relationship research, the experts themselves differ in how they view gender differences in friendship. One group, I'll call them the *Dividers*, has arrayed lots of data demonstrating the persistence and reliability of differences between men and women in their close relationships. John Gray used their data to depict a wide chasm between the relationship ways of men and women.

On the other side are aligned the researchers who argue men and women actually don't differ that much in their close friendships. I'll label this group the *Uniters* since they tend to emphasize the similarities in men's and women's close relationships.

Most interesting, these two groups often cite the same data to bolster their cases, suggesting the two perspectives are probably more complementary than antagonistic. Like a lot of controversial issues, it boils down to a matter of spin. Or putting it in terms of the statisticians, it depends on the amount of variance in the data associated with the gender of the research participants.

I'd like to look at the research on both sides of the issue as objectively as I can, beginning with the *Dividers*.

One dramatic difference

The *Dividers* often cite one particular survey item that seems to capture a key difference between men and women's friendships. This question has appeared on a variety of research questionnaires (including my own) over the past 25 years: If you were forced to choose between "doing some activity" or "just talk" with a same-sex close friend, which would you choose?

The gender differences on this item are quite dramatic. For example, in one study nearly four times as many women as men prefer to "just talk." In the messy, highly varied and often contradictory world of relationship research, this difference is outstanding. And over the 25 years this question has been posed to college students as well as respondents of all ages and walks of life, little seems to have changed despite the clear evolution of gender roles in our society over that same period.

The dichotomy posed by this question symbolizes what the *Dividers* see as a fundamental difference between the same-sex friendships of men versus those of women. Men like to do things with their closest friends, while women prefer just talking with theirs. And women's talk more often is of the self-disclosing, supportive, relationship-oriented variety. When men talk, the topics typically concern things external to their relationship, such as sports, politics, or issues related to their work.

Women love their best friend of the same sex about as much as they love their opposite sex lover; men do not.

–Robert Sternberg

The *Dividers* often cite a second, related finding: Women reliably rate their friendships as more satisfying than do men. This is likely a side effect of women's talk, which tends to be more supportive and emotionally oriented. This difference has been found in a number of studies using a variety of surveys and methods.

So the primary argument of the *Dividers* boils down to these two issues: Women talk more, especially in emotionally expressive and supportive ways, and they typically rate their friendships as more satisfying. Men prefer the camaraderie of doing things together, having fun, but they also rate their friendships as less satisfying.

Does science perpetuate stereotypes?

The *Dividers* like to express these distinctions graphically, referring to women as cultivating "face-to-face" friendships compared to the "side-by-side" friendships of men. These labels conjure up an image of two women sitting at a table in a coffee shop, with heads bent in toward each other, totally immersed in their conversation, while two men have their eyes glued to the TV set, waiting in tense anticipation for the outcome of a critical fourth-down play.

I can hear some of you groaning—haven't we outgrown these simplistic ideas about men and women? Apparently not, since even rather recent studies produce large differences on those two key issues of relationship talk and relationship satisfaction.

What men want

Some might argue men prefer their friendships with other men to be devoid of any emotional talk, whether or not it is supportive in nature. Male friends feel close by spending time, the camaraderie of doing things together, which brings feelings of loyalty and solidarity. They save their emotional needs for their wives, or other women in their lives. Studies support this view: Married men or men in close relationships with women tend to be less emotionally expressive in their interactions with other men.

The great question that has never been answered, and which I have not yet been able to answer, despite my thirty years of research into the feminine soul, is what does a woman want?

–Sigmund Freud

Researchers specializing in adult development claim that women share their intimate exchanges with both their husbands and their best women friends. They cultivate both kinds of supportive and satisfying relationships. Husbands, on the other hand, confine all of their intimate exchanges to their wives, a bit like putting all of their emotional eggs in one basket.

No drama please

However, when researchers ask men to describe their ideal friendship, they quite often include the ability to talk about anything and feel supported by the friend. There are several different versions of these studies, and they all point to the idea that most men would like to have some emotional expressiveness in their friendships with other men. Yet they don't seem to behave accordingly. So the question is, why?

Relationship researchers often refer to the "emotional restraint" of men's friendships, the fact that they tend to hold back in their emotional exchanges with other men. Some of these studies refer to it as homophobia, fear of appearing effeminate or homosexual. But when I look at the actual items measuring this construct, it seems to entail much more than heterosexual men's fear of appearing gay. Men, generally speaking, are simply not comfortable expressing feelings with other men.

Another reason often cited for this restraint stems from what society rewards and does not reward in young boys and the men they grow up to become. According to this view, men are not reinforced by society for expressing weaknesses, vulnerabilities or personal problems. It's the big-boys-don't-cry norm. Society in general, including women of course, do not find these behaviors in men very attractive, and men expressing these sentiments do not gain positive social attention.

Boys and men are systematically reinforced by society for wearing an invulnerable coat of psychological armor. But spending time with close friends should represent a timeout from the demands of society, a time to put the armor aside. Confidential surveys suggest this is what men want in their ideal friendships. But in reality, they often can't handle it.

Historical perspectives

Emotional expressiveness in men's friendships has an interesting history. For ages, in fact, male friendships were romanticized, often portrayed as the ideal relationship, rhapsodized by the Greeks and other philosophers down through the centuries. During most of recorded history, men's friendships were considered far more important and meaningful in a man's life than his relationship with his wife.

Even in the U.S. in the 19th and early 20th century, men were quite expressive of their affections with their men friends, as evidenced by the numerous photos of men holding hands or the intimacy and love expressed in letters between male friends. Some might say these were latent (or even expressed) homosexual relationships, but history proves them wrong in the vast majority of cases. Even ultra-masculine

Theodore Roosevelt openly expressed affection in his many letters to men friends.

So what has happened to change all that. Why are the men of today so restrained? Historians and behavioral theorists often cite competitive sports and the cutthroat business world, as well as homophobia as potential explanations. My point here is simply that men weren't always this way.

The catty-woman stereotype?

Some of you might be wondering about the common stereotype of women's friendships as seething with competition, conflict, and gossipy backbiting. Often making headlines are stories of adolescent girls inflicting all sorts of cruelties on each other, either directly or via social media such as Facebook.

In perusing all the major reviews of the research literature on adult friendships, this stereotype never surfaces. Digging deeper, it is possible to find individual studies on things such as conflict, gossip and competitiveness. But even in these cases, the results suggest gender differences are either minimal or, more frequently, non-existent. Results suggest that men can be just as competitive and gossipy as women. We have to conclude the female version of this stereotype is completely overblown.

I think women know how to be friends. That's what saves our lives

–Alice Adams

If there were any validity to it at all, one would expect women to prefer friendships with men rather than other women, and on average, that is not the case.

Dealing with conflict

Dividers often cite one aspect of expressiveness as an additional point of difference between men's and women's approaches to relationships. It concerns how we deal with conflict. Both genders have ways of avoiding conflict in their friendships, but overall, women are more likely to have a heart-to-heart talk, where everything is brought out in the open and discussed, and where each is more likely to end up feeling understood and supported by the other.

By contrast, studies suggest men are more likely to bypass interpersonal conflicts simply by setting these issues aside and avoiding any direct talk of them. Men's approach to sports is often seen as exemplifying this strategy.

While there is ample evidence for these ideas, it's worth noting that social researchers see conflict avoidance as unhealthy for relationships in the long-term. It can breed resentment, perhaps explaining why men rate their friendships as less satisfying.

Summarizing the *Dividers' arguments*

Studies have shown rather consistently that women's friendships revolve around talk, especially supportive talk that leaves them feeling a sense of connectedness, while men's friendships tend to be more activity oriented, having fun doing things together. For men, closeness develops from their sense of solidarity and camaraderie, not from sharing their emotions. Women rate their friendships as more satisfying than men do, primarily because of their felt connection. Lastly, women, compared to men, seem more capable of dealing directly with conflict in their close friendships.

The challenge of the *Uniters*

Let's now look at the other camp, the *Uniters*, who argue men's friendships really don't differ much from those of women. They have a much harder time making their case even though more of the data fall in their favor. The problem revolves around the scientific difficulty of proving a negative, in this case, demonstrating that there are no significant differences between the friendship habits of men and women. The way the research and publication world functions is also part of the problem.

Let's say, for example, we did a very rigorous study, measuring ten core aspects of close friendships and found that for nine of these measures, men's and women's friendships don't differ. (In fact, this is often the case.) The way research works, that one aspect demonstrating a significant difference between the friendships of men and women will attract all the attention, and is much more likely to get published.

This rule applies to popular media as well. Findings of no difference never make headlines, whereas talking about Venus and Mars, and men going into their man-caves, now that sparks the imagination and boosts viewer ratings!

A plethora of ignored findings

Regardless, what follows is a thumbnail sketch of a variety of research findings showing little or no difference between men's and women's friendships.

Most importantly, men and women tend to be in strong agreement about what they value in a friendship. Both want friends they can depend on, who are loyal, and friends they can trust. Both want to feel free to talk about anything, even personal matters or problems they might be experiencing, and know the friend will respond supportively. Both cite the importance of having fun with friends, engaging in some activity they find enjoyable, sharing their lives, feeling connected, and knowing each is there for the other in times of need.

A bogus distinction

Yes, *Uniters* admit, men on average will respond differently than women when forced to choose between "doing some activity" or "just talk" with a same-sex friend. But that's an unrealistic scenario—when was the last time you faced such a choice? Typically we do some of each with our friends. We all cultivate friendships that revolve around doing things in specific settings, such as tennis friends, work friends, friends we worship with, neighborhood friends, movie friends, or going-out-to-eat friends. And when we're together, we talk. The distinction between talking and doing things is artificial at best, they argue.

Data are never simple

The claim that women talk with their friends and men don't is riddled with exceptions. Take, for example self-disclosure, talking about very personal matters, which the *Dividers* often cite as an area where men and women differ most widely. There are numerous studies that cloud this distinction.

For example, single men have been found to be much more likely to engage in self-disclosure compared to married men. Young men self-disclose much more than older men. Men who score high on androgyny (having characteristics stereotypic of both men and women) self-disclose more than gender-stereotypic men. The topic also matters— men are more willing to self-disclose about some issues compared to others.

The type of methodology used in the research can be a factor: In one study, college students were instructed to talk with a friend about how their relationships with family members had changed since they left home for college. Under these conditions, men actually self-disclosed more than women. Apparently, being instructed to self-disclose provided sufficient motivation to relax the emotional restraint thought to characterize male friendships.

Uniters also like to point out that self-disclosure plays only a very minor role in most everyday interactions with close friends, and this is true for both men and women. Self-disclosure is a critical factor early in developing friendships and can arise again during periods of difficulty, when one of the friends is facing a major life challenge and is seeking solace from the other. But in ordinary everyday life, the need to self-disclose is mostly irrelevant to the functioning of the friendship.

I could go on with more such findings. The point is even the most prominent gender difference in close friendships, emotional expressiveness, has numerous qualifications and exceptions. Let's now turn to the issue of relationship satisfaction.

Men with satisfying friendships

Some men do report highly satisfying friendships, and relationship researchers have looked at this group carefully to see what makes them tick. They are more likely to score higher on androgyny, feeling comfortable with both stereotypic male and female characteristics. These are heterosexual men who show little sign of homophobia. They tend to be supportive of gay rights and gay causes, for example.

Love does not consist in gazing at each other, but in looking outward together in the same direction.

–Antoine de Saint-Exupery

Another factor involves the role models boys observe growing up. If young boys see their fathers cultivating close friendships with other men, spending time with them, sharing important moments of their lives, these boys will have similarly satisfying friendships when they are adults. This is such an obvious finding it hardly seems worth mentioning, but the effects are powerful and lasting.

These men do cultivate friendships for doing things together and having fun, but for them, these occasions provide opportunities to go beyond fun and games. Feelings and expressions of support often get exchanged in the process.

These emotional exchanges may not necessarily be the face-to-face, full-throttle, let-it-all-hang-out emotional therapy sessions that, stereotypically speaking, seem to characterize at least some women's friendships. Nevertheless, emotions do get communicated, sometimes indirectly, sometimes with humor, sometimes with an offhand comment that might leave some details unsaid. Men who rate their male friendships highly do have their social and emotional needs met in these relationships.

Closeness and man-talk: A personal example

My own close friendships with other men seem to run the gamut when it comes to emotional expressiveness. I have one friend who is quite comfortable discussing his feelings and does so often, while others are more restrained.

With one close friend, a guy I've known for 40-plus years, we rarely talk openly about our feelings. In most respects, our friendship fits the stereotypical model of male friendships touted by the *Dividers*. Our common interests include politics, history, astronomy and cosmology, not exploring each other's emotional lives.

Yet, I would argue, we share a very strong emotional bond. We have each had our difficult moments over the decades of our friendship, and during these stressful periods, we have been pillars of support for each other. These personal difficulties, like a financial setback or a serious health problem, tend to be discussed rather factually. We make little explicit reference to the feelings we are experiencing. Yet, the emotional power of these moments is unmistakable. I always feel his empathy and support. Plus, his keen sense of humor helps me put any problem in perspective. He has a terrific talent for finding the ludicrous absurdities in life's most trying moments!

Relevant to this discussion is another perspective raised by many who study gender differences in friendships. They argue that measures of relationship closeness and satisfaction tend to be based too much on expressive talk. They claim this is a female definition of closeness and satisfaction, and that men have different ways of feeling close to a friend. Simply doing things together, working on a common project, accomplishing some challenging feat or just having fun—can't these be indicators of closeness?

Going back to this same friend, over the years, we have pooled our talents on a number of home improvement projects. We've built room additions, porches, tool sheds, and decks. These are difficult and arduous projects, requiring days, sometimes weeks, of working side by side. There is no better way to appreciate the measure of a man than to do manual labor with him. And for the years that follow, each and every time I make use of one of our collaborative accomplishments, I think about what a terrific friend I have!

Demography matters

One way of putting both sides of this argument in perspective is to look at demographics. This research allows for the following conclusions: Gender differences in close friendships are quite minimal among young adults, those who live in urban settings, who are well educated, at least middle class, and have androgynous personalities. By contrast, gender differences tend to be greater among older adults, those living in more rural settings, who are working class with less education, and have gender-stereotyped personalities.

Even these conclusions should be seen as tenuous. As the sociologist Ray Pahl has noted, gender roles are evolving quite rapidly. The behavioral norms for men and women of my childhood bear little resemblance to their norms of today. Any conclusions we draw about differences of men's versus women's friendship will probably have little relevance to the friendships of tomorrow.

Ray Pahl also points out, and other researchers concur, any gender differences that do exist in close friendships tend to diminish with the maturing of the relationship. Friendships that have existed for years show almost no measurable gender differences.

If you doubt these conclusions, I ask you to spend a few moments thinking of all the friendships in your network of acquaintances, those of both men and women. It is likely that you will note a very wide range of differing styles of male friendships and an equally wide range of female friendships. At least in my experience, any rule about gender differences would have to be highly qualified with multiple exceptions. In most respects, when it comes to friendships, men and women really don't differ much at all.

Cultures, gender and friendship

So what about gender differences among friends in other cultures? Geert Hofstede measured the extent of gender role differences in 53 different nations and regions around the world. In countries with stronger gender differentiation, men and women tend to be more segregated in society, and it would be reasonable to expect greater differences in their friendship patterns.

The U.S. scored 15th on this scale, implying that gender role expectations differ more in the U.S. compared to 38 other nations or regions. (When I first read this finding, it came as a big surprise, since I have tended to think of the U.S. as a leader in gender equality. That may be true in the legal realm, but when it comes to the equality of our roles in society, we're still more differentiated than many countries of the world.) Since the evidence for gender differences in friendship is minimal in the U.S., based on the research I reviewed above, we shouldn't expect major differences in men's and women's friendships when we examine international data. In fact, that is what I found.

Gender and the six styles of friendship

In the case of *Interveners* versus *Independents*, I found no evidence at all of gender differences in the cultures I studied. Men and women were equally likely to hold the two views: Either that it was their duty, their responsibility, to take care of their closest friends or that friends should respect each other's autonomy, and not interfere in each other's lives. None of the cultures I studied came up different on these two styles.

Inferences from my data and those of others suggest that men tend to favor the *Includer* style, while women the *Excluder* style. This suggests men are more likely to project a friendly exterior and demonstrate their social skills for superficial interactions more than women. Women are more likely to make clearer distinctions between their friends versus their acquaintances, and their social skills for closeness allow them to feel more comfortable spending extended periods of time with the same friend.

I've also concluded that men tend to favor the *Idealist* style, and women, the *Realist* style. This suggests men are more likely to exaggerate the positive qualities of their friends, have concerns about issues of face, and thus try to avoid directly confronting friends on important issues. Women are more likely to see both the positive and negative qualities of their friends, and are less concerned with matters of face, which allow them to speak more frankly with their friends, even about sensitive issues.

I hasten to add that the differences I've just outlined are quite small, accounting for only a tiny portion of the variability in the measures. Thus they are relatively unimportant, and not consistent across cultures.

Once again

However, there was one area in my results that showed a very clear gender difference in close friendship, and this difference was consistent across cultures. As you may have already guessed, women in my studies place much more importance on the role of expressive talk in their close friendships compared to men. In statistical terms, one's gender is three times more strongly associated with verbal expressiveness scores compared to one's cultural background. In plain English, this implies that women's friendships depend very significantly on intimate talk, much more so than do the friendships of men, and this gender difference is consistent across cultures.

Despite the strength and pervasiveness of this finding, again there are exceptions that must be considered. For example, relationship researchers are keen to cite a study that compared the self-disclosure patterns of friends in the U.S. to those in India. They found the usual gender differences among friends in the U.S., but little or no such differences among Indian friends. Apparently, men in India, generally speaking, feel less restraint in expressing their emotions compared to men in the U.S. (Given the tremendous cultural diversity in India, I'm sure there are exceptions to this finding as well.)

Cross-sex friendships

What about friendships between men and women? I wrote an entire chapter about this topic in a book edited by Robin Goodwin and Duncan Cramer entitled, *Inappropriate Relationships*. In it I explored the down side of cross-sex friendships, which can easily become exploitive since men tend to contribute less and gain more in these relationships.

There are also clear advantages to these friendships that are cited often by researchers working in this field: Having friends of both sexes can double our number of potential friends, provide us insider information about the opposite sex, improve our understanding of the other sex, and serve to validate our attractiveness to the opposite sex, to mention just a few.

I've done a number of studies on cross-sex friendships with Donna Webster Nelson and found that these friendships tend to showcase gender differences in very complex ways. In one series of studies, we looked specifically at men who prefer women as close friends as well as women who prefer men as close friends.

We found that women who prefer men as their closest friends tended to cultivate a style of friendship that would fit the stereotype of male friends. They appreciated having less "drama" in their friendships, simply having fun, and pursuing common activities and interests. Similarly, men who prefer women as their closest friends tended to appreciate the feelings of connectedness that result from more expressive and supportive talk.

One important finding is these studies was that once we considered preference, gender differences in relationship satisfaction completely disappear. The point here is this: If you are in a friendship that fits your preference, i.e., preferring one gender over the other as close friends, you tend to be quite satisfied, whether you are a man or a woman. In this case, there are no gender differences in friendship satisfaction.

It's up to you

Throughout this book, I've argued that what it means to be a close friend is defined in part by the culture in which we grew up. In this chapter, I've tried to show how gender influences our friendships, although that influence may not be as pervasive or dramatic as the older stereotypes of men and women would suggest. It's better to think of the gender differences that do exist as stylistic in nature. And to repeat my favorite refrain, we can each chose a style of friendship that fits us best.

For most young people today, gender is simply not much of an issue in their closest friendships.

Looking ahead

And younger people are changing a lot of other things about how we conduct our friendships. In the next chapter, I'll examine online games, Twitter, and especially Facebook, trying to answer the question of what they have to do with friendship. The answer may surprise you—at least, it did me.

Chapter 13

What is real about virtual friendship?

The split between the virtual and real worlds is no longer relevant.

–Alexie Navalny, Russian blogger, commenting on the role of Facebook in organizing anti-government protests in Moscow, as quoted by *Time Magazine*, 15 January 2012

Try to guess this event: Tickets were $175 each and they sold out in seconds, over 20,000 of them. Ticketholders came from all 50 states and 49 countries, and they'd been anticipating this event for years. They just wanted to hang out with their friends, with whom they'd banded together many times in the past to overcome major adversities.

Throngs of adoring fans surrounded the stars, but there were no bodyguards—everyone held nothing but the warmest affections for each other, even though all of them spent a significant portion of their day-to-day lives engaged in combat. The oddest thing about this crowd is that the majority of them had never met face-to-face before.

So what was this most unusual gathering? It was a convention put on by Blizzard Entertainment for players of their online games *World of Warcraft* and *StarCraft II*. According to the NY Times article describing the event, the players continued to hang out long after the convention was over, like a bunch kids at the close of a fantastic summer camp. They just couldn't say their good-byes.

Facing my biases

No doubt, how we relate to our friends is changing very rapidly. With cell phones, text messaging, online games, and social networking sites such as Facebook, LinkedIn, and Twitter, our relationships are more and more mediated by new technologies. This chapter is about what these phenomena actually have to do with friendship.

I'm trying to make the world a more open place.

–Mark Zuckerberg

The more that people are willing to put online, the more money his site can make from advertisers.

–Jose Antonio Vargas, writing for The New Yorker, 20 September 2010

I have to confess, I initially approached this topic with some deep-seated anxieties. At that point, I was not on Facebook, LinkedIn or Twitter, I'd never played an online game, and to be honest, I'd always harbored a slight prejudice against these forms of socializing, mostly because I saw them as sad substitutes for the real thing.

So when I first began this research, I decided, for the sake of this book, to join Facebook since it represents the primary online social phenomenon that intends to be about friendship. I hoped that doing so would help me appreciate what all the fuss was about, and allow me some first-hand experience concerning the research literature I'm about to describe. At the end of the chapter, I'll let you know if my opinion has changed.

The deluge of research

Searching through the research literature on new media (as they call it) has been eye-opening. There are new journals, with terms like Cyberpsychology in the title. I was overwhelmed by the sheer quantity of research, just trying to wade through it all. I suspect many of the dissertations being written today in social psychology and communications are focused on these new media. I also suspect those graduate students are teaching their professors a thing or two about connecting in today's world. And their research is aimed at such a frenetically moving target—it's all evolving as we breathe!

I'll direct most of my comments toward Facebook because of its stated focus on friendship but include a few findings about other social media when it's germane.

The Facebook world

Facebook is everywhere! Even in countries with little access to the Internet, those few who can log on are nearly all signing on to Facebook. A few countries have their own social networking websites such as Cyworld in South Korea, Orkut in Brazil, Renren in China, and Vkontakte in Russia, but many have simply signed up for Facebook.

Facebook now has 500 million users. The previous record holder was heroin.

–Jimmy Kimmel

The phenomenon is occurring world wide, and its impact extends well beyond college students and their friends. The 2008 and 2012 elections in the U.S. and the popular uprisings in the Middle East were markedly influenced by Facebook, Twitter and other social media, providing an effective platform for their activist voices.

With Facebook, I have had to learn a new vocabulary: friending and unfriending (establishing and disestablishing an online contact), updating my status (writing about what I've been doing lately), and liking (indicating my approval of another's site or post).

748 Facebook friends

But what does Facebook have to do with close friendships? Well, according to much of the research currently available, it turns out Facebook has quite a lot to do with friendship. Obviously, it is easy to have a jaundiced view of the connection between Facebook and friendship when you hear that people have hundreds of friends.

Indeed, Facebook friends are not the same as close friends as I've been using the term in this book, and Facebook users will readily admit that. Among their Facebook friends are family members, distant relatives, coworkers, old high school and college friends one hasn't seen in decades, neighbors, former neighbors, and on and on. One's close friends may be on the list, but buried in a myriad of others.

Friendship researchers, initially at least, viewed Facebook with unbridled skepticism. They felt then, and still feel, it cheapens the term "friend," and contributes to the perception that USAers are shallow. If the founders of Facebook had employed a more neutral term, like "contacts," which is used in so many other contexts, I think much of this controversy could have been avoided. Or they could have done like the Korean Cyworld social networking website, and coined their own term, *ilchon*, which is typically translated as "cyber buddy."

There are now scores of studies assessing all aspects of the Facebook phenomenon, leaving us with a rather clear picture of the role it plays in users' lives. I'll focus initially on research by the Pew Internet & American Life Project, because their work seems to be the most comprehensive and convincing.

How amazing to be able to tell your 1,344 closest friends, 'guess who I saw at the Apple store? I died it was so awkward!!!!!!!'

–Katie Roiphe, a cartoon in the 13 August 2010 issue of The New Yorker

Given the ubiquity of Facebook, the first result surprised me. They found that, for the average USAer, most of their contact with close friends is still face-to-face rather than computer mediated. In other words, friends of today spend time doing the same things friends have always done, sharing coffee or a meal, engaging in mutually interesting activities, or just hanging out. At this point at least, Facebook doesn't appear to have changed the fundamental habits of close friends.

In an alienated world

Other research shows that the core social networks of people in the U.S. have shrunk by a third since 1985, mostly due to a loss of friends. The rates of social isolation, people feeling like they have no one in their networks with whom they can discuss important matters, have increased markedly over the same period.

The Pew research has confirmed these trends but has also found something that appears to be a recent reversal. In the last few years, USAers' social networks have actually increased rather than decreased. It is too soon to tell if this trend will continue, but it is noteworthy that these data were collected during the time of burgeoning popularity of Facebook, Twitter, and other social media.

Pew researchers have also shown that users of Facebook are less likely to feel socially isolated. They have more close confidants, referred to as "strong" ties, with whom they can discuss important personal matters. Several Pew studies now have drawn the conclusion that Facebook tends to support friendships rather than undermine them.

Facebook benefits

Facebook generally increases one's sense of feeling socially supported, of having friends one can count on. Researchers have various ways of measuring social support, and Facebook is associated with higher levels of all of them. It is worth emphasizing this point, because the difference between Facebook users and non-users on these measures of support is quite large, statistically equivalent to "half a spouse," and spouses are rated as the greatest source of personal support.

Call it a clan, call it a network, call it a tribe, call it a family: Whatever you call it, whoever you are, you need one.

–Jane Howard

Facebook users tend to be at ease socially. Spending all this time, and Nielsen ratings suggest USAers spend a lot of time on Facebook, leaves one with very positive feelings about one's social environment. Users are much more likely than non-users, for example, to agree with statements like, "Most people can be trusted."

What type of person is most attracted to Facebook? As you might expect, they tend to score higher on things like extroversion and narcissism. Many Facebook users are highly social people to start with, and joining Facebook merely allows them another avenue to express their social tendencies.

At least one study shows that Facebook also appeals to those who are painfully shy, people who would like to have friends but feel awkward in social settings. These socially anxious individuals use Facebook to compensate for their limitations.

How we spend our Facebook time

Research shows that the majority of our time on Facebook is spent maintaining existing relationships, rather than making new friends. Users visit each other's sites, "liking" their content, checking out each other's photos, etc. On average, people less frequently update their status, which again is cyber-speak for writing about what one has been up to lately, although there's tremendous variation on this count, with a few people reporting nearly every event in their day-to-day lives. Older people use it to keep up with family and pursue a common interest or hobby.

Like-minded isolationism

One idea often floated in news media these days is that USAers are becoming more and more polarized in their attitudes and values. People avail themselves of news media that are already consistent with their beliefs and attitudes, and Facebook has taken some of the blame for these trends. By surrounding ourselves with people who are quite similar to us, the argument goes, we are never exposed to a wider variety of perspectives, especially with points of view opposing our own.

Whether it's treating a customer badly or gross abuse of state power, the always-on generation will make its voice heard—on Facebook, Twitter, YouTube or on the streets.

–Mark L. Clifford, writing in Time Magazine, 10 January 2012

Research has examined this issue very carefully, and most (but not all) have concluded that the social networks of Facebook users and non-users are about equally diverse. Indeed, users often comment on the complications of dealing with their contacts who have conflicting political or religious beliefs, and Facebook has responded with new privacy settings, which help manage these issues. But it's probably not fair to say that Facebook contributes to political polarization.

I should hasten to add that Facebook is clearly related to political activism. Users are much more likely than non-users to vote, attend a political rally, and try to persuade others to vote as they do. There are lots of other ways to measure civic engagement, and in most cases Facebook users are more engaged than non-users. Neighbors with their own Facebook page are more responsive to neighborhood concerns.

Strength in numbers

In the most recent Pew research, the average Facebook user has 207 contacts. (Now really, isn't it better to use the term "contacts" here, rather than "friends?") Other studies have put that average much higher, somewhere between 300-400.

Researchers view most of these as "weak" ties, people we know and love but whom we don't consider as part of our core network of family and close friends ("strong" ties). Nevertheless, we do derive clear benefits from these weak-tie networks. Being widely connected can boost our morale, but more importantly, it can provide a variety of knowledge, skills and resources we can call on if necessity dictates.

If I were diagnosed with a serious disease, chances are good someone in this network knows someone who has experienced the same thing and can provide first-hand knowledge that might prove helpful. Researchers cite this factor as the reason why Facebook usage is related to various measures of wellbeing.

The weak-tie network research applies to Twitter as well. We don't befriend others on Twitter, we "follow" them, and one's following can provide the same advantages as any weak-tie network. Twitter and its equivalents in other countries have also been linked to social and political movements around the world. Twitter, especially, can be a way to get the word out when reporters can't enter war-torn areas.

Cultivating our brands

When I first joined Facebook, I found it interesting that among the myriad buttons I could click to describe myself, nowhere was there a button for ethnicity. Well, apparently, this hasn't discouraged many Facebook users. By their photos, food preferences, appreciated quotations, and other information they post, users demonstrate it is quite okay to be ethnic on Facebook.

Posting information is like pornography, a slick, impersonal exhibition.

–William Deresiewicz

In the real world, many of us tone down our ethnicity in order to fit in. Facebook is one place where we seem to let it all hang out, allowing users to learn about each other's culture and ethnicity. As one who values social diversity and cross-cultural understanding, I see this as yet another advantage of Facebook.

My epiphany

Up to this point, all my comments about Facebook have been highly positive. What about my initial misgivings, my belief that Facebook actually represents a false version of spending time with friends? Well, my careful and objective examination of the research has led to a change of heart. I've found no convincing evidence that Facebook takes us away from real contact with friends and family. In fact, Facebook appears to strengthen both strong and weak-tie networks.

The dark sides of Facebook

This is not to say that Facebook doesn't have a downside. It most certainly does, and it is to that topic I turn next. There are a lot of negatives, in fact, but I'll cover them relatively briefly, not because they're unimportant, but simply because they are less relevant to friendship. Besides, most of these factors are already well known.

Friendship should be a private pleasure, not a public boast.

-John Mason Brown

An issue that came up often is the violation of users' privacy. Facebook intends to make major profits, of course, so your personal information is routinely sold to advertisers. They've even admitted violating their own privacy agreements on occasions.

Users are often responsible for their own loss of privacy. Some Facebook users, especially young men, post photos or information about themselves they later come to regret. This information can be used against them in child custody cases, by potential employers, or in other contexts where their reputations are at stake.

Facebook and falling in love

Facebook both facilitates and complicates the lives of dating singles. Lovers often start as Facebook contacts, allowing each access to lots of information about the other. As the relationship develops, partners continue to peruse each other's sites—and this isn't considered "spying," not like peeking into their closets or reading their emails. Publicly announcing their love on Facebook serves to solidify and validate their relationship. But if their romance fails, the tragedy plays out dramatically and painfully on the Facebook stage, with family, friends, coworkers, and acquaintances all watching in the audience.

Facebook can also cause serious conflict within romantic relationships. Spending lots of time on Facebook, contacting former romantic partners, revealing personal information about problems in their relationship have all been mentioned as sources of conflict for couples, and have even been cited as grounds for divorce.

Jealousy is all the fun you think they had.

-Erica Jong

No time for academics

Nearly all college students are on Facebook, many having it on throughout the day, hovering in the background on their computers. So it shouldn't come as a surprise that heavy usage is associated with lower grades, in fact, much lower grades. But research has looked at this issue in detail, and found that those who simply log on to see what others are up to, plan out their social lives, and share links with others actually get higher grades than average. The students with real problems are those who use it to chat online and constantly post status updates. More time spent in these Facebook activities is associated with considerably lower grades.

You created a profile for your kitty.

-One of David Letterman's top 10 signs you're obsessed with Facebook

Living or cyber living

If you are a Facebook user, you've probably noticed that a few people spend an inordinate amount of time constantly adding updates, commenting on others' posts and engaging in all manner of exchanges. Research suggests that some heavy usage fits the pattern of an addiction, not unlike drug or alcohol dependence.

They're simulacra of my friends, little dehydrated packets of images and information, no more my friends than a set of baseball cards is the New York Mets.

-William Deresiewicz

They log on out of a sense of loneliness and feeling disconnected from others. While online posting status updates and reading and commenting on those of others, they experience some temporary relief from these symptoms. Yet this reprieve is very transient. Even after prolonged time online, as soon as they log off, the negative feelings return. Over time, this pattern becomes habitual and the core problems, loneliness and feeling disconnected, grow even worse.

Like any addiction, Facebook grows into a daily compulsion, taking up more and more of the user's time, leading them to shirk responsibilities, as parents, at their work or other obligations. As I am writing this, I discover a plethora of websites devoted to Facebook addiction. Ironically, every one of them included a "like" button!

Cyber bullying

All of the research on cyber bullying focuses on high school students, where bullying has been an issue since time immemorial— what online media have done is simply exacerbate the repercussions. One child insults another online, the second child can take revenge instantly, and within nanoseconds the entire school can get caught up in the conflict. At what point the exchange constitutes bullying is difficult to define or litigate. What is clear is the ease and power of such taunting, thanks to social media.

At least bullies of previous decades had to hold you down before they could spit in your face.

-Time, 2010, Vol 176, Issue 16, p 60.

As I hope you can readily see, there are lots and lots of negatives to online social media.

Cultural variations

Although there weren't many studies, the most fascinating thing I learned preparing for this chapter was how other cultures use social media. Since the Facebook platform is identical everywhere around the world, a study comparing usage across cultures on this one medium would constitute the perfect cross-cultural study. Unfortunately, that study has yet to be published. I'm sure some industrious graduate student is doing her or his dissertation on this very topic as we speak.

The few studies that have been published provide some intriguing findings. Here's a sampling based on a 2012 Forrester Research report: Italians are twice as likely to engage in social networking compared to Germans. The Japanese tend to shun Facebook because it requires users to give their real names, whereas Mixi, a popular Japanese site, doesn't have such a requirement. People in the U.S. and Western Europe are more likely to be passive users of Facebook, compared to people in emerging economies who tend to create more social content, such as posts, photos, music and blogs. Chinese Internet users are among the heaviest users of all social media.

From a 2010 Pew study, there isn't a significant difference in the number of men versus women who use social networking sites throughout the world, with three exceptions: In the U.S., women subscribe significantly more often than men, and in Turkey and Japan, men outnumber the women. Given their inclination for the *Includer* style of friendship, it isn't surprising that USAers list the largest number of contacts, five times as many as South Korean users, for example.

"Cying" in South Korea

South Koreans make for a colorful comparison to U.S. users. In many respects, Koreans have been international trendsetters for all forms of electronic communication. They had pagers, cell phones, high-speed broadband in their homes, and social networking sites years before they became popular phenomena in the West.

Their most popular social networking site is called Cyworld, a term that plays off both the concept of cyberspace and a Korean word ("cy") for "relationship," or literally, "between." Cyworld resembles Western social networking sites, but there are notable cultural differences. An early study, before Facebook became popular in the U.S., referred to Cyworld as "a relaxing hangout" compared to MySpace, which was described as "a hip party where users vie for popularity and attention."

Is there a site that streams the World Cup final online? (I don't own a TV.)

–Mark Zuckerberg, writing on his Facebook page

Cyworld is a clear reflection of many aspects of Korean culture. Korean users place a lot of importance on designing their home pages to make visitors feel welcome, by creating the right ambiance or mood (the concept of *kibun*), by the type of music triggered automatically when a visitor arrives and by the background images or "skins" decorating their homepages. Gift giving permeates every aspect of Cyworld.

Korean wall posts echo the assumption that all close relationships are predestined, a fortuitous matter of fate rather than something they could actively control (the concept of *yon*). Many posts imply the cultural value of *noonchi*, the art of interpreting any text at different levels, the ability to read between the lines, to gain deeper meanings of what is being said.

Other examples

People in India and China tend to use social networking sites as sources of information—where USAers might use Google or Yahoo, these cultures put more stock in their social networks as providers of reliable information.

Also reflecting their more collectivist cultures, Asians tend to prefer multiparty chat groups to one-on-one scenarios. They use lots of emoticons, those little smiley or frowning faces and other symbols that provide another channel of communication, analogous to non-verbal forms of communication in the real world.

Socializing in a virtual world

I must say a word or two about online simulations like *Second Life* and games such as *World of Warcraft*, that I mentioned when opening this chapter. Millions of users participate in these virtual realities. I found their popularity shocking! Even more surprising is the fact that when relationship researchers examine these phenomena with the same tools they use to study relationships in the real world, in many cases, they are indistinguishable.

That is, these online relationships embody the same characteristics as their analogue counterparts in the real world, such as high levels of trust and support, companionship, solidarity, and affection. Support groups in *Second Life* have been shown to be very beneficial for people facing cancer or struggling with an addiction.

The Internet social advantage

Another surprising finding about these online simulations and games is how easily users develop a rapport with others online. Since they often don't see their online communicants, they don't have the full gamut of interpersonal cues as in face-to-face interactions. So they imaginatively, if unconsciously, fill in the gaps in ways fulfilling their expectations of what they hope for in a friendship.

Like the *Idealist* style of friendship, we tend to approach any online relationship with idealized notions of who this person is, and what this person means to me. Thus supportive online relationships can be very supportive indeed, and there are now lots of studies demonstrating the genuine nature of these friendships.

Having fun with Facebook?

So what about my own attempt to join the Facebook phenomenon? Given all the positive things I'd been reading in the literature, it wasn't hard to approach it with an open mind. In fact, I felt a genuine sense of excitement setting up my Facebook page and receiving requests to "friend" people in my real life social circle. I especially enjoyed looking at their Facebook pages, their photos, learning about recent vacations, music they enjoy or the latest recommendation on a cool restaurant. It's been fun!

But even after a several months, I still feel some anxiety each time I log on, and I've been at a loss to explain exactly why. Then a friend sent me an article by William Deresiewicz. I have read some rather scathing critiques of Facebook over the past months, but nothing as eloquent, moving and thought provoking as this one. Deresiewicz genuinely captured the essence of my malaise with Facebook.

Like Deresiewicz, Facebook has accentuated the fact that there is nothing circular about my circle of friends. Each comes from a very different segment of my life. I have friends from my times in Paris, Seoul and New York, a friend that dates back to graduate school days, a friend with whom I regularly play handball, a friend I go clubbing with to hear live music, friends from the university, and friends whom I met through my wife, who is an active artist. Most of these people don't actually know each other.

When I'm with each of these individuals, I tend to adjust what I say and how I say it depending on who they are, their individual interests, personalities, and most of all, the nature of our friendship. (Research suggests this is not an uncommon phenomenon.) It is no exaggeration that, in fact, I'm a slightly different person with each of these friends, a result of our common history and the very unique, personal rapport we create each time we're together. I simply can't imagine having my friends in the same room at the same time—Yikes! I wouldn't know who I am!

And this is precisely the dilemma I face each time I log on—I find it confusing to "talk" to all my friends as a collective. I tend to freeze, trying to imagine how my posts are being received by each of them.

There is really nothing very personal about conducting one's personal relationships on Facebook. Experienced users have told me this self-consciousness will pass—I hope they're right about this. At this point, I spend most of my Facebook time reading other's posts rather than adding to the conversation.

Friends and contacts

All of which brings me back to the bigger question, what does Facebook have to do with friendship? My own experience has been consistent with the research. Facebook hasn't diminished the time I spend with my friends or how I feel about them. I've grown to realize that Facebook is, as the label suggests, a social networking site. It isn't so much about friendship as it is a way of keeping up with people you know and love from all corners of your life. I already have several contacts I haven't seen in decades, and I've been enjoying reading their posts and learning about their current lives. It's also been a convenient way to keep up with family members, all of whom live at a distance.

One former colleague, whom I haven't seen in years, has made a genuine art of the way he uses Facebook. His posts do occasionally comment on things going on in his life, but more frequently, they represent some humorous insight, a unique idea or perspective, perhaps a social or political commentary, but often something thought-provoking or profound. Without Facebook, I wouldn't have regular access to this friend.

Looking ahead

The last chapter encourages us to take a step back and look at all the potentials of our close friendships, as well as potential friendships.

Chapter 14

Friends beyond borders

Go oft to the house of thy friend, for weeds choke the unused path.

-Ralph Waldo Emerson

Well, have I succeeded in getting you to think about your closest friendships in ways you hadn't considered before?

I hope so. From the very beginning, that has been my overarching goal in writing *Friends Beyond Borders*. By describing cultural variations and the differing styles of close friendship, I hope you've come to find examples of each of these approaches among your own friends. I've tried to shed some light on these contradictory assumptions about friendship that can so easily lead to confusion and frustration. My wish is for you to see your friends with new eyes and renewed enthusiasm, and to feel inspired to invest more of yourself in your closest friendships.

Friends as clones

Both extensive social research and common experience suggest that we are most likely to nurture friendships with people who are quite similar to ourselves, similar in terms of attitudes, values, interests, ages, socioeconomic backgrounds, and a whole host of other factors. Although we can all come up with obvious exceptions to this norm, in fact, we tend to hold as our closest friends others who, in so many respects, are veritable clones of ourselves. This can be very reassuring and comforting.

It can also be quite limiting.

Life is partly what we make it, and partly what it is made by the friends we choose.

−Tehyi Hsieh

In this final chapter of *Friends Beyond Borders*, I'd like to urge you to resist this trend, to leave yourself open to friendships that go beyond these artificial and confining boundaries. There's clear evidence that many young people of today are already defying this norm. Their closest friendships embody a great deal of diversity, ethnically, racially, in terms of gender and along other dimensions as well. If the rest of us would follow their example, I argue, we'd all lead richer, more fulfilling lives.

Crossing cultural borders

I've had a few life-changing events in my past, but in retrospect, the most impactful turning points were making French, and subsequently Korean, friends.

As opportunities present themselves, I encourage you to open yourselves to friendships with people from other cultures, if you haven't already done so. In the beginning, it may feel a bit like you are bridging some cosmic chasm, trying to understand and be understood by

It is as though when we come in contact with our friend we enter into a different environment.

−Andrew M. Greeley

someone from a vastly different world. But simply making time, learning about, and caring about someone who grew up and thinks differently can enrich your life in so many inestimable ways.

My friendships in South Korea and France have transformed many aspects of my life; especially how I see the world that surrounds me and my role in it. I could speak at length on this topic, but suffice it to say this broader perspective, a cross-cultural perspective, impacts nearly every aspect of my day-to-day reality. If wisdom can be defined as seeing things from a variety of points of view, then having close friends in other cultures can make one the wiser for it.

At a more practical and fun level, having friends abroad to visit from time to time, getting an insider's perspective on a culture, can be so much more enjoyable, enriching, and rewarding than traveling as a tourist, a stranger in a strange land, staying in impersonal hotels, just there to see the sights.

These friends can also help perfect your foreign language skills, and becoming comfortable in another language provides a whole other set of rewards.

If you are a USAer, you have the distinct advantage (and disadvantage) of being the focus of a lot of attention around the world. People already know a lot about our nation, our history, and our culture, and with that comes a curiosity about us as people. Many would love to know us as individuals. I hear this sentiment often.

The way our friends interpret us helps us to interpret ourselves.

–Ray Pahl

Elisabeth Gareis, a friendship researcher at Baruch College, has documented repeatedly, and I've found this to be the case in many of my own interviews, that internationals are often frustrated in their attempts to make friends with USAers. Whether they are immigrants or sojourners, they arrive in the U.S. with a clear intention of making new USAer friends, and initially at least, respond very positively to the open, friendly demeanor of many USAers. But after a time, they feel something is missing. Their friendly overtures aren't returned in ways they think of as constituting real friendship.

So the potential is clearly there for USAers; it's simply a matter of being open to the opportunities. This may require learning to appreciate a different version of friendship, which brings us to the second set of borders worth crossing.

Friendship styles

Having a friend who holds very different assumptions about what it means to be a close friend can be enormously fulfilling, allowing you to experience a version of friendship you may not have known even existed. Referring back to the six styles of close friendship that form the primary focus of this book, it is important to appreciate how incompatible these versions of friendship can be: *Interveners* versus *Independents*, *Excluders* versus *Includers*, *Realists* versus *Idealists*.

Using the expression "versus" between each pair of styles is no accident: They really are quite contradictory in how they would define a good friend, making it so easy for each to misinterpret the friendly intentions of the other. The overt, well-intended gestures of the *Intervener* can feel invasive and too controlling to the *Independent*, whereas the wordiness and simply-having-fun orientation of the *Independent* may appear shallow, insincere, or even contrary to genuine friendship to the *Intervener*.

Friendship is like a prism through which the many variations of beauty are revealed in our lives.

–Anonymous

Similarly, the blatantly promiscuous friendliness of the *Includer* appears showy, shallow and insincere to the *Excluder*. The cool detachment of the *Excluder* seems snobby and can discourage any interest in friendship on the part of *Includers*. The frank talk of the *Realist* can feel like a putdown, whereas the overly positive, supportive talk of the *Idealist* seems artificial and disingenuous.

Of course, these differing styles of close friendship are most noticeable when you cross cultural borders, but I'm sure you can note gradations of these styles even among your local friends. I applaud your attempts to understand and appreciate these differences, all the while keeping an open mind about potential friends.

Wishing to be friends is quick work, but friendship is a slow-ripening fruit.

–Aristotle

For many USAers, this may require developing an appreciation for a different version of friendship, one that values some interdependence, some occasional interventions, perhaps franker talk, talk that isn't simply intended to stroke each other's egos, and it may also require making clearer distinctions between friends and mere acquaintances. Close friends are special people, and they expect to be treated as such.

For non-USAers

I also have words of encouragement to those of you who were not born in the U.S. To succeed in making friends with USAers requires you to be open minded as well about other versions of friendships. USAers who are self-disclosing personal information are opening themselves up to exploring the possibilities of close friendship. You must learn to read those signals. And it is important to encourage these revelations, to reciprocate in kind, to find common ground in your beliefs and values, all in a conversational context that emphasizes the positive.

USAers are capable of close and very satisfying friendship, but at least initially, it may require a clear emphasis on providing supportive and encouraging words, of sharing the fun side of life.

It also requires persistence. Speaking from personal experience, I've witnessed close and endearing friendships develop between USAers and internationals. More frequently, I've seen these relationships have problems making it past a clear tipping point where both parties see their relationship as an enduring friendship.

In my experience, to make friends with USAers entails repeated exposure over an extended period of time to come to fruition. And once established, these friendships should never be taken for granted.

How often we find ourselves turning our backs on our actual friends, that we might go and meet their ideal cousins.

–Henry David Thoreau

International student advisors who work with students coming to U.S. campuses sometimes advise them to lower their expectations if they are to have fulfilling friendships with USAers. This may be true if they expect to end up with an *Intervener-Excluder-Realist* style friendship that may have been the norm in their home cultures. If this applies to you, I would like to encourage you to see the value of another version of friendship, one that can be equally satisfying if pursued faithfully and with an open mind.

On the other hand, one could argue it is the USAers who need to lower their expectations since, as I claim in Chapter Eight, they have a tendency to idealize these relationships. As Joseph Epstein has argued so persuasively, those idealized notions of friendship can be patently counterproductive. No friend can live up to those expectations. We are all flawed human beings. Real friendship begins where these idealistic notions leave off.

Friendships across gender borders

I'd like to advocate for friendships that cross other borders as well. Men and women can be friends, and these friendships can prove to be enormously satisfying for both parties.

I encourage men to take special care in their friendships with women. Ample research suggests that men tend to give less and take more from these relationships, and this lopsided arrangement can render them less satisfying for women. Friendships function best when both parties cultivate, respect, and value the relationship equally.

For many, public perceptions and sexual tensions can complicate these relationships, especially when they are seen to compete with one's romantic relationship. But when handled with sensitivity and care for all concerned, these tensions can be managed, and in fact, can render these relationships more interesting. One must keep all parties' best interests in mind. Of course, one could argue this rule applies equally to all manner or style of friendship.

Sexual orientation borders

Gays, lesbians, and transgendered individuals are out of the closet to stay, and their fuller integration into our daily lives has led to a more open and accepting society, where everyone feels free to breathe a little easier. When I look across cultures, it's possible to find other cultures that are more accepting and promoting of diversity—especially the variations in sexual orientation—compared to the U.S., but not very many.

Friendship is the only cement that will ever hold the world together.

-Woodrow Wilson

Given our nearly maniacal obsession with political correctness, our laws protecting the rights of minorities of all kinds, and our attempts to provide equal representation at the seats of power for all subgroups in our culture, we can feel proud of the progress we've made, while remaining mindful of the work still to be done.

This social progress has been slower in the realm of close friendships. This is another area where younger people are clearly leading the way. Their acceptance of one's sexual orientation as a non-issue can be seen in their social habits, which include friendships between straights and gays and among all other variations of gender and sexual orientation. While exceptions can be found, they mostly evidence a very open, accepting approach to these issues.

People who've crossed this border in their social lives all tend to make the same observation, that one's sexual orientation simply melts away as a factor once they know each other as individuals.

The last frontier

I would like to take my encouragement of border-crossing friendships one step further, into relatively uncharted territory, to include crossing ideological boundaries. This is a step, I must confess, I've yet to take myself. But I've felt a need for some time, and plan to make it happen in the near future.

Genuine tolerance does not mean ignoring differences as if differences made no difference. Genuine tolerance means engaging differences within a bond of civility and respect.

–Richard John Neuhaus

You hear it so often it has become an understatement: We are living in an ever more polarized world. Increasingly, we divide ourselves up and segregate ourselves socially according to our ideas, our beliefs, and our values. We tend to confine our social lives to the company of like-minded people. Friendships that cross these ideological lines, spending time with and caring about people who think differently than we do about religion, politics, or social issues can surely benefit those of us who make the effort as well as our entire communities. It's something to think about.

Making time

Like a lot of older folks, I've found it easier to spend regular time with my closest friends since retiring. But like people of all ages, I haven't always had that luxury. It's easy to allow other priorities to displace the roles of friends in our lives.

Fear less, hope more; eat less, chew more; whine less, breathe more; talk less, say more; hate less, love more; and all good things are yours.

–Swedish Proverb

I'm sure many of you struggle with balancing these competing priorities as well. You may be at a point in your life where all of your relationship energy is devoted to your spouse, your children and your career, with very little time or energy left over for friendship. I encourage you, even if you have the busiest of lives, to make regular time for your closest friends, if only just a 30-minute coffee break once a month. And when you're together, let your friend know how important this time is.

Men, especially, are apt to let their friendships slip away from them when the demands of family and career are at their highest. And then, later in their lives, when they actually have the time, they've forgotten how to be a good friend. I've surveyed and interviewed these men, and nearly all of them regret their circumstances. Their relationship lives are truly impoverished.

A final wish

My advocacy of friendships that cross borders reflects my grander belief in the value of allowing our close friendships to play a central role in our lives. I'm not suggesting we recreate the mindset of the early Greek philosophers, who rhapsodized thoughtfully, endlessly, about virtuous men and the love and affection that characterize their perfect friendships.

In reality, friends can be annoying, an emotional burden, rendering our lives more complicated, sometimes even adding to our stress. Real friendships exact their price. But I contend the benefits greatly outweigh the costs, especially when we give our friendships deep consideration, conduct them with unambiguous intention, and allow them more gravity in our lives.

I'm speaking of friendships that can rival our romantic relationships for our personal wellbeing. Of course, these friendships will play out quite differently for each of us, depending on our personalities and how we express closeness and caring for another human being. In the end, it boils down to knowing that someone enjoys my company, someone cares, someone wishes the best for me, and that all these feelings are mutual.

Close friendship requires time and effort. And friendships that cross any of the borders described here require even more time and effort, in addition to an open mind. I hope the research and ideas presented in this book have made it easier and more satisfying for you to cultivate friends beyond borders.

If you've stuck with me to this point, it's probably fair to say that we share at least some small bond of friendship as well. I would love to have your reactions, to hear your friendship stories, especially if they concern aspects of these relationships I haven't mentioned. I answer all my emails (**Roger@friendsbeyondbordersbook.com**). Please write!

Appendix

Odysseys in methodologies

Man is rated the highest animal, at least among all animals who returned the questionnaire.

–Robert Brault

This appendix is mostly about statistics and methodology, so I'm very surprised you are actually reading this!

In fact, I taught statistics and/or methodology almost every semester during my thirty years at Winthrop University, and never managed to get students to like or even just appreciate the importance of these subjects.

I tried, I so tried!

And I never got jaded. Each semester I would enter a class of fresh faces with full optimism this time would be different, this time students would see the importance of these concepts, the value of understanding more precisely how psychology functions as a science.

But in reality, the most I could ever get from them was tolerance, begrudging tolerance.

So this is why I'm so surprised you're reading this. But I'm glad you are, and I'll do my best to make it worth your ride! What follows details my struggles of making the transition from memory researcher to cross-cultural researcher, beginning with the concept of culture itself. In many ways, it is a story of my life.

The myth of USAer culture?

When I present my friendship research in public, one response I often get from USAers is the claim that we in the U.S. don't really have an identifiable culture. We are a country of immigrants, they argue, a genuine mixture of a very wide variety of ethnicities and cultures.

How can you possibly lump us all together as one culture, especially given the many regional variations that are readily evident in different parts of the U.S? After all, what do Charlotteans and Manhattanites have in common, culturally speaking?

In this appendix I hope to explain and defend some of the assumptions underlying cross-cultural research as well as the methods used by researchers to gain a better understanding of the influences of national cultures in our lives.

Yes, regions of the U.S. do have their own distinctive cultures. This fact was brought home to me in a very real fashion when I moved to South Carolina from Ohio in the early '70s—I suffered a severe case of culture shock! But that's another story, one that would take us way off topic.

Discovering one's own culture

On the other hand, thinking the U.S. doesn't have its own identifiable culture is a belief one loses very quickly after living abroad for any length of time at all. For example, students in the U.S. talking about their study abroad experiences often confess the biggest lesson they learned was what it means to be a USAer.

Our democracy, our culture, our whole way of life is a spectacular triumph of the blah.

–P. J. O'Rourke

Anyone who has worked with students studying abroad has heard that sentiment many, many times. Only when we have to cope with living in another culture do we fully grasp the nature of our own culture. Only then do we appreciate the power and pervasiveness of cultural influences in every aspect of our day-to-day lives.

Arguments for a USAer culture can be made from a variety of perspectives. Even our outward USAer appearance alone reflects our very distinct culture. During my first year abroad in the late '80s, it always astounded me that total strangers in Paris would know, even before I opened my mouth, that I was a USAer. At one point, I became obsessed with this issue—what gives me away? How do they know?

Whenever I discussed this phenomenon with my French friends, they always referred to my "tête américaine," my American face or head, which they saw as a dead give-away. They also mentioned clothes, including shoes, the way we walk, and our tendency to speak louder than necessary. So for a while, I tried to dress European, walk like a European, I even wiped that indigenous USAer smile completely off my face, hoping to disguise my "tête."

I spent my days walking around scowling!

Eventually I got to the point of confusing at least a few people. It didn't happen often. But it felt like a major accomplishment each time it did. For example, once I helped a young woman out on the street who couldn't get her moped started—she asked if I would push while she peddled. I did and it fired up within seconds. Before we parted, she asked my nationality, was I German? I said, "No, I'm an American."

"Oh, capitalist!" she shouted over the roar of the engine, then laughed heartily and zoomed off in a noisy haze of blue smoke.

Research and USAer culture

The idea that we USAers are so diverse as to not have our own unique culture does have a lot of intuitive appeal. However, there are very convincing data implying a set of cultural values that dominate USAer thinking regardless of our ethnic backgrounds, the region where we live, our age, or even our social class.

One way of approaching this argument is to look at the data gathered by the World Values Survey Association, an international group of social scientists who attempt to track cultural changes in all of the nations of the world over time. They provide convincing arguments that cultures can be examined at the national level. You can learn all about them at www.worldvaluessurvey.org.

Unlike most researchers in the field who keep a tight rein on their raw data and methods, this group takes a completely transparent approach to their work. Any researcher can access their surveys to see the specific questions they use, examine their data sets, do their own analyses, even publish their own findings if they so wish.

This group has some very interesting things to say about how cultures around the world are changing over time. If you have traveled at all, it would be easy to conclude that lots of cultures are becoming "Americanized," with McDonald's, Starbucks, and KFC outlets seemingly on every corner of all the major cities of the world. But according to the researchers at the World Values Survey, the picture is much more complicated than that.

One trend they document throughout the developing world is away from traditional/religious values toward what they refer to as more secular/rational ones. That is, developed cultures around the world are becoming less spiritual or religious and more likely to value scientific data or other more concrete bases for their thinking.

Our value is the sum of our values.

-Joe Batten

Because the U.S. has maintained strong religious beliefs, much stronger than most developed countries, it doesn't appear to clearly reflect this global trend toward secularism. So these world trends don't suggest everyone is becoming Americanized. Rather, as the cultural values of the world evolve, they seem to be trending more toward Northern Europeans. Perhaps, we're all becoming a bit more like the Swedes.

The World Values Survey Association looks at cultural values at a national level and their data provide a very strong defense for this approach, clearly showing an identifiable set of cultural values that can be used to characterize each nation. That is, their results show that people within any nation have much in common, despite regional, religious, ethnic, tribal and socioeconomic differences.

For example, in terms of their cultural values, Muslims in Nigeria have more in common with Christians in Nigeria compared to Muslims in India. Similarly, a very wealthy person in Germany, in terms of cultural values, has more in common with a very poor person in Germany compared to a wealthy person in neighboring France.

Their data clearly show the validity and power of examining cultures at a national level. Over and over, with a wide variety of measures, they show that cultural variation within nations is much smaller than variations between nations. This is not to say that ethnic variations within a country don't exist. They most certainly do, and they can be the source of great strife, sometimes leading to the breakup of nations, such as Yugoslavia, for example. But overall, nations do have common and identifiable values that can be used to characterize them as a culture.

Characterizing USAer culture

So it is empirically defensible to think of USAer culture, despite all of our regional and ethnic variations. In addition, as I described in Chapter Three, major cross-cultural studies by Geert Hofstede, Shalom Schwartz, Fons Trompenaars and many others have compared the responses of thousands of people in dozens of nations. They have been able to plot out the cultural norms and values of each nation, including the U.S., creating a kind of empirically-based stereotype of USAer culture.

If man is to survive, he will have learned to take a delight in the essential differences between men and between cultures. He will learn that differences in ideas and attitudes are a delight, part of life's exciting variety, not something to fear.
–Gene Roddenberry

USAers tend to score high on measures of individualism (valuing the individual over the collective), mastery (assuming one can control most factors in one's life as opposed to more fatalistic assumptions), masculinity (prizing accomplishments over quality of life issues), egalitarianism (assuming all are created equal versus respecting social hierarchies) and I could go on. There are dozens of these empirically developed dimensions. And these values tend to characterize us as a nation, regardless of whether we live in Charlotte, Los Angeles, New York, or on a farm in rural Ohio.

This is not to say that cultural variations within the U.S. aren't interesting and important, and worthy of study. I'm especially fascinated by cultural differences that stem from socio-economic factors. Annette Lareau of the University of Pennsylvania has done some of the most interesting work in this field, especially the ways in which these differences show up in child-rearing patterns. Joseph White, Thomas Kochman, and George Henderson have each documented insightful cultural differences between African Americans versus European Americans.

Despite all of our variations, we in the U.S. have a lot that draws us together as a culture: A common language, our numerous media (TV, movies, music, YouTube, Facebook, various news sources, print media), our elections, the ease of travel, sports teams, our institutions of higher education, just to name a few. It is true that the Internet and social media have done much to foster communications across cultures around the world leading to mutual understandings and a sharing of cultural values. Yet, as the World Values Survey research has shown, one's nationality still remains a powerful indicator of one's cultural values.

Methodology and cross-cultural research

Let's now look more specifically at my attempts to do cross-cultural research, focused on cultural differences in close friendships. Recall from the introduction, my interest in cultures and friendships resulted from a sort of midlife crisis. My original graduate training was in memory research, all of which I conducted in laboratories, in soundproof booths, using very precise measures of reaction times as volunteers responded to previously memorized information.

Research is what I'm doing when I don't know what I'm doing.

–Wernher von Braun

When it came to cross-cultural research, I was truly a beginner, naively thinking I could simply construct a questionnaire about friendship, translate it into a few languages, and then figure out ways to administer it to groups of volunteers in various countries. I had so much to learn!

Starting from the beginning, one fortunate decision I made was to configure my questionnaires such that volunteers focused their responses on a specific close friend, rather than responding on the basis of their generic ideas about friendship. I asked them to think of one particular friend, someone they saw as a very close friend, and to respond to all of the questions as they would apply to this particular friendship. I felt this strategy added real-life validity to their responses, rather than drawing on abstract notions of friendship.

When opportunities would arise, I also did a limited amount of interviewing of individuals about their close friendships. I followed a similar strategy of asking the interviewee to focus on a specific close friend and then I would ask questions about this particular friend. To my regret later on, I was never very disciplined or systematic in my interviews—I would try but rarely succeeded in adhering to a prescribed rubric. I often allowed the interviewee to take the lead in telling me all about this specific friendship, how it evolved, the role it played in his or her life, perhaps talking about crises in the friendship that were memorable.

On several occasions when I was abroad, I was allowed to visit college classrooms where English was being taught and engage the students in a discussion of what it means to be a close friend. In both the individual and the group settings, I viewed my role as the gatherer of these friendship stories rather than a systematic interviewer.

Friends, not lovers

I was much more disciplined and scientifically sensitive regarding my questionnaire research. To begin with, I took steps to ensure that the friend they were referring to was not also their lover, since we, especially in the U.S., tend to think of our spouse or romantic partner as a close friend. I made this distinction clear in the instructions as well as including an item later in the questionnaire that served as a "validity check." (This question asked them to rate their romantic feelings about this close friend. Those who gave anything but a clearly negative response were excluded from the study.)

From a relationship research perspective, romantic relationships have a set of characteristics, such as feelings of exclusivity and possessiveness, which are less relevant to most friendships. In the research literature on close relationships, all studies attempt to be clear about such distinctions.

Getting lost in translations

The first major challenge I encountered was the translation process itself. I assumed that hiring a professional translator, a specialist, someone who makes his or her living on a day-to-day basis doing this kind of work, would result in a valid translation of my questionnaire.

I quickly learned, even with my amateur level of French, that several of the questionnaire statements in the French version were not precisely equivalent to my original English version. For example, the original English statement, "When we have a conflict, usually one of us wins out over the other" came out in the French version literally as, "In case of a difference, one of us always wins out over the other." I was bothered by losing the concept of "conflict" as well as substituting "always" for "usually." I felt it changed significantly the meaning of the original English statement. To my frustration, I found many such discrepancies.

Cross-cultural researchers have developed methods to ensure the equivalence of questionnaire items across languages and cultures, and I had much to learn about developing these techniques. Focusing on the translation process itself, they use a method requiring a "blind back translation" performed by a second translator who specializes from French to English, and who has never seen the original English version. I would then compare the translated English version to the original in search of discrepancies.

If we knew what we were doing it wouldn't be research.

-Albert Einstein

When discrepancies occurred, sometimes it was simply a matter of finding a more appropriate French translation, and when such a version could not be developed, it was necessary to rewrite the original English version to make it more translatable. In most cases it took several rounds of these back translations to develop a functional version of my questionnaire. And this had to be done for each language. This task alone was enough to cause me feelings of regret, tempting me back to the nerdy, controlled methodology of a memory researcher!

And it gets worse. Professional cross-cultural survey constructors have some very sophisticated statistical techniques to determine the functional equivalence of survey items across cultures. They are able to plot, in a multidimensional statistical space, the responses to a set of survey questions from a variety of cultures. If a survey item occupies the same multidimensional space in a variety of cultures, it is thought to be functionally equivalent. Since I was more interested in exploring cultural differences in people's notions of close friendship rather than the construction of measurement scales, I did not apply these techniques to the extent that would have been ideal.

Getting lost in connotations

Even when items were translated very precisely, there are differences in the connotations of key words that must be considered. For example, the words "dependent" and "independent" have almost opposite connotations in English compared to most East Asian languages such as Korean or Japanese. The word "independent" carries mostly positive connotations in English, and more negative connotations in Asian languages. The opposite is true for the term "dependent."

Subtler differences can be found with many other words. A questionnaire item such as "My friend is very intelligent" can carry implications far beyond one's grades at the university. Many languages employ the same word for "intelligent" and "well behaved." In English, we clearly separate those two concepts—a child, for example, can be seen as intelligent and a holy terror in the classroom at the same time.

To push this issue a step further, even when the connotations of a given questionnaire item are quite parallel across languages, respondents still may interpret it differently for social-psychological reasons.

Take one item I had on a very early version of my questionnaire, "I would not hesitate to ask this friend for help." I assumed that strong agreement with this statement would imply that the respondent could depend on the friend for assistance when needed. Based on the work of Raymonde Carroll, this assumption could be false. In some cultures, if one needs help and has to ask for it, without the friend first volunteering, would imply there is something wrong with the friendship. In these cultures, a sign of a close friendship is not having to ask for help when needed—good friends pitch in without being asked. So in this case, a positive response to that item would imply a less helpful friend.

All of these challenges render the study of cultural differences of any sort a very imperfect science, especially compared to the laboratory research I had done for the first half of my career. I learned that cross-cultural researchers must do a number of studies, measuring their constructs in a variety of ways before they feel comfortable drawing strong conclusions.

In addition to these cultural issues, there are other limitations to using surveys and questionnaires as tools for understanding people's friendships. These instruments ask for people's opinions, their perceptions, how they think about their close friends. They don't (and can't) measure what actually transpires in these friendships. There is no way to circumvent this problem, but it is an issue that must always color our interpretation of survey results.

Friendships are never one-sided affairs

Friendships involve at least two people and surveys and questionnaires tend to reveal only one perspective on any given friendship. Until very recently, it was extremely rare among relationship researchers to gain both perspectives in a friendship.

Advances in statistical techniques have allowed researchers to view the responses of both members of a friendship as the basic unit of comparisons. And the advent of miniaturized electronic devices similar to smart phones as well as responding via websites has facilitated the collection of such data. Unfortunately, these advances occurred well after I had collected the data I am citing as the basis for my conclusions in this book.

In classroom discussions of friendship I have conducted in the cultures I was surveying, including the U.S., there were a few times when both parties in a friendship would approach me after the session to tell me about their relationship. I always found their comments fascinating, but the total number of times this occurred was quite small, perhaps a couple dozen in all, not enough to garner any systematic conclusions.

As an aside, examining both perspectives in a given friendship often produces thought provoking findings. Lillian Rubin looked at platonic friendships between men and women, and on some occasions, she was able to sequentially interview both partners in a friendship. However, one of her findings was that some women whom men classified as "close friends" reported the feelings were not mutual. Yes, the women said, they knew the men in question, and in most cases, saw them as nice guys, but certainly didn't think of them as close friends. So if she had had only the perspective of the men, she could have easily misrepresented the nature of their relationships.

Regardless, the survey research that forms the bulk of my findings is based on only one perspective for each of the friendships I was studying. It was simply one of many tradeoffs one makes in doing cross-cultural research.

When a 6 is really a 7

When it came time to actually gather questionnaire data, I also discovered some major complications on how different cultures respond to questions on these instruments. This led to a whole new set of methodological headaches.

My questionnaire worked like this: Each item was in the form of a declarative statement, such as "My friend is very intelligent," followed by the numbers 1 through 7, where 1 represented strong disagreement and 7 strong agreement. Taking this example, let's say the average French response was 6 and the average Chinese response was 5—may I conclude that the French, on average, see their friends as more intelligent than do the Chinese? No, not at all.

Numbers constitute the only universal language.

–Nathanael West

One major problem with such direct comparisons is that cultures use the 1-7 response scale, rating their level of agreement, very differently. Cross-cultural research has shown, and my data were no exception, that the Chinese (as well as other East Asians) tend to be rather conservative in their overall response patterns. Avoiding extremes, moderation in all things, is an Asian value, the result of many historical influences, especially the role Buddhism has played in Asian thought.

Thus, most of their responses hover around the midpoint of the scale, in this case a 4. If they agree with the statement, they might circle the 5, or if they strongly agree, they might even dare to circle the 6. Both 1's and 7's were relatively rare responses on my questionnaires in both China and South Korea. Quite the opposite would be the case in the U.S. and France. Their questionnaires tended to have many responses at the extremes of the scale, 1's and 7's. So the average Chinese response of 5 about how intelligent they saw their close friend may actually have reflected stronger feelings of agreement than the average French response of 6.

Those disagreeable French

We refer to the Asian response patterns as reflecting a conservative response bias, and this factor has been systematically studied across many cultures. I had to deal with other kinds of biases in how different cultures use a seven-point scale. USAers, for example, tend to be very "agreeable" when responding to such scales. That is, their responses tend toward the positive (agreement) side of the scale.

While the questionnaires I used changed and evolved over time, the average USAer response was always on the positive side of the scale, around 4.60. The French, by contrast, responded in a more negative fashion, with an average response slightly below 4.0. East Asians had average responses very close to the middle of the scale.

I hope you see the point that a cross-cultural researcher may not make direct comparisons when cultures differ so dramatically in how they use the seven-point response scale. I would not be measuring them with the same yardstick. In fact, each person, regardless of culture, responds to these scales somewhat differently. These differences have to be statistically "corrected" before making comparisons across cultures.

Happily, in this case, there is a rather simple, elegant solution to the problem of response biases. All of my questionnaires (aside from the vignette studies described below) involved a very large number of items, often over 150 seven-point scale responses. This large number of responses allowed me to assess each respondent's individual response biases and thus correct for them, putting everyone on an equivalent scale of "agreeing" and "disagreeing."

Statistics, the great equalizer

Technically, this is accomplished by having the computer calculate each person's average response score over all of the items, and then converting each response into a new score relative to one's overall average. If you have ever taken a course in beginning level statistics, you will recognize these as "standardized" scores, also referred to as Z-scores.

A man's friendships are one of the best measures of his worth.

–Charles Darwin

It essentially evaluates each response relative to that person's overall pattern of responding. Responses above one's average would be positive numbers, indicating a stronger level of agreement, and numbers below one's average would be negative numbers, indicating less agreement. Computers perform such calculations in the blink of an eye!

So now, when I compare the Chinese and the French on an item like "My friend is very intelligent," I am comparing the average Chinese response (relative to their overall tendencies toward agreement/disagreement) to the average French response (relative to their overall tendencies toward agreement/disagreement), allowing for a much more fair comparison. (After such a correction, the French still scored higher on this particular item.) "Correcting" survey data in this fashion represents an overall loss of variability, making it more difficult to find any differences across cultures. One could view this as an advantage, since differences that do make it past this higher bar probably have meaningful implications in the real world, beyond the realm of statistical abstractions.

My friend gets all 7s

There is one more issue about respondents' use of the seven-point scale that also has a rather simple, standard fix. If a respondent is very enthusiastic about his or her friend, there is tendency to repetitively respond with 7s to all items, even without fully reading them. This positive response bias can cloud important distinctions between the various underlying aspects of close friendships I was trying to measure.

This response pattern can also be triggered by respondent fatigue, especially with long, detailed questionnaires like mine. To deal with this issue, nearly all questionnaires have some items worded in the negative, such as "My friend isn't very intelligent." Of course, these items are scored in reverse, with low numbers indicating the respondent thinks of the friend as intelligent. My questionnaires always had a sufficient number of these items included to keep the respondent from answering without carefully reading each item.

Looking for the bigger trends

All of these issues urge us be quite careful with interpreting the results of any single item on a questionnaire. Typically, we feel more comfortable when a variety of items are pointing to the same conclusion. And there are some rather standard procedures for assessing the extent to which a group of items is measuring the same underlying concept.

For example, I had several items trying to assess the closeness of the friendship. Since these items are aimed at measuring the same construct, their responses should be very similar. They should produce a consistent pattern of responses. To assess whether or not they are similar, we use some very simple statistical measures of the internal consistency of a group of items. These items must reach a certain level of inter-correlation to render the measure scientifically acceptable.

The college student as cultural representative

To the extent I was able to respect all of these factors, I constructed a questionnaire and translated it into multiple languages. The next challenge was getting people from various cultures to respond.

The ideal would be to have representative, matched samples from each of my target cultures. The science of developing representative samples is quite well-developed, as can be witnessed in the accuracy of political polling data in predicting subsequent elections. Again, the realities of limited budgets require one to settle for much less than the ideal. (Understandably, science foundations or other funding sources don't see research in cultural differences in close friendships as a high priority!)

Since I viewed my work as largely exploratory, I was content to settle for samples that could be considered approximately equivalent across cultures, even if they were not fully representative of each culture studied. I fell back on the strategy employed in most social-psychological research: I recruited samples of university students.

A university professor set an examination question in which he asked what is the difference between ignorance and apathy. The professor had to give an A+ to a student who answered: I don't know and I don't care.

–Richard Pratt

I did this via colleagues I met at cross-cultural conferences, professionals who developed an interest in my research and were willing to take my questionnaire and administer it to groups of university students in their own respective countries. I also visited France, Spain, South Korea and Cuba, where I had opportunities to both administer my questionnaires and interview individuals and groups of students about their friendships.

I also administered my questionnaires and interviewed many international students studying in the U.S., representing a total of thirteen different countries. Clearly, university students and their friendships are not fully representative of their native cultures, but they do allow us to see a range of possible friendships, especially when these differences vary systematically between cultures.

University students hold a rather consistent stature within each culture. They are, by and large, young adults, living semi-communally, often away from home, and for whom friendships are an important aspect of their lives. It is the best I could do to find relatively equivalent samples in a variety of cultures.

Students with attitude

One aspect of my investigations that is troubling, and this applies to nearly all cross-cultural research, is the fact that respondents enter into their task of completing the questionnaire with very different levels of motivation. In South Korea, for example, simply because I was a "professor" and a "social scientist," most university students were quite cooperative and enthusiastic about completing my questionnaires. They were always eager to participate. It was an eye-opening experience for me to spend time in a culture where professors and other educators are treated with such respect!

This attitude contrasted sharply with what I experienced in France, for example, where students often started my questionnaire, but given that it took them at least 30 minutes to complete, they often wouldn't finish it. I received a significant number of incomplete questionnaires, which I had to discard. As a result, I suspect these varying levels of motivation influenced my findings in ways I cannot assess. The motivation levels of the participants in all cross-cultural research confound the results in ways that can't be easily avoided.

And now, for something completely different

Later on in my career as cross-cultural researcher, I develop a technique that did not require long questionnaires, thus avoiding many of their shortcomings. I made up short vignettes, stories that depicted critical events in a friendship, and then asked respondents in various cultures their opinions about those events and how the friends behaved. It was a way of asking them how they thought about a normal, healthy friendship without asking them about their own friendship experiences.

One such vignette discussed earlier concerned two close friends, one a very serious student bent on getting the other, her partying friend, to toe the academic line. Students in five different cultures rated this friendship along various dimensions measuring how normal or healthy they saw this relationship. I used this study to infer some cultures' preference for the *Intervener* style of friendship, where actively intervening in the life of a close friend is considered normal and healthy.

Joshua Searle-White did a similar study comparing students in Russia and the U.S. In his vignette, a friend asked Joe (or Jane) whether he (the friend) could stay in Joe's tiny apartment, just for a few days. Joe says ok, but then when the few days were up, the friend asks to stay a week longer. The question was, should Joe allow this incursion into his space, or should he resist. Searle-White found that Russian students saw the incursion as more acceptable compared to students in the U.S. I would interpret his finding to imply a greater acceptance among the Russian students for the *Intervener* style of friendship, where actually doing things to help the friend is considered the norm.

Is it all worth it?

There are many other complications and challenges of doing cross-cultural research, but I hope this sampling of key issues gives at least a taste of the trials and tribulations of these endeavors. After reading about all the various ways things can go wrong in this research, it is reasonable to ask whether or not the scientific approach has much to offer our understanding of cultural differences in close friendships.

Or is each friendship such a unique and personal phenomenon that any attempt to understand it from a research perspective is doomed to failure? If you are still reading at this point, I suspect, or at least hope you have found some merit in the empirical approach to understanding these important relationships.

Looking ahead

I have lots and lots of people to thank, in the acknowledgments that follow.

Acknowledgments

So many to thank

It is daunting to think about all of the people who have helped me with my research and writing along the way. I'm sure to forget some of the names. If you are one of those who've contributed to this endeavor and you don't find your name below, I'm so sorry!

As per the dedication at the very beginning of this book, I owe a heartfelt thanks to all the university students and people of all ages who completed my various friendship surveys over the years. I am especially grateful to a smaller subset of you who spent time with me recounting your friendship stories.

Of greatest benefit were those international students at Winthrop who volunteered each semester to share your personal experiences with me as you tried to make new USAer friends while on campus. Your stories have greatly influenced my thinking. There are a few of you I'd love to mention by name, but given my promises of confidentiality, you'll have to remain anonymous.

There were many professionals who served to guide me as I retooled in what was an entirely new field of research for me. Others helped with administering the questionnaires, analyzing results and providing feedback on my attempts to publish the findings.

Starting from the very beginning, I owe much thanks to Gary Ferraro, whose many books have helped thousands in the world of international business. He was my first mentor, guiding my early readings, helping me get oriented in the field of cross-cultural research. Patrice Bruneau helped with survey construction and French translation issues in early versions of my questionnaires. His extensive computer skills rescued me in times of sheer panic while coping with vexing technological glitches.

Nami Lee is a South Korean psychiatrist who served as my mentor to all things Korean. Her encouragement and interest in my research opened a multitude of doors, providing me with translations of my instruments, introducing me to experts on Korean culture and helping me gain access to a variety of university students who served as participants in my research. Her insights and expertise regarding Korean culture are well documented in her many best-selling books. Our lengthy discussions of these topics have strongly influenced my ideas about the nature of close friendships in South Korea. I feel very privileged to have Nami as a dear friend.

Frank Concilus provided me with an anthropologist's perspective on Korean culture and allowed me to visit his classes in Seoul, carry on lengthy discussions with his students and seek volunteers to participate in my research. He introduced me to others who helped me in similar ways.

Kinga Kerekes single-handedly arranged for multiple translations of my surveys in Romania and gathered data from a variety of settings in her culture as well. Kathy Lyon of Winthrop University and Steve Kulich of Shanghai International Studies University helped with administering my surveys in China. Steve also provided lots of insights and feedback about cultural aspects of close friendship in Chinese cultures. Rita Olga Martínez and Carlos Lloga Domíngues gathered survey data in two regions of Cuba.

Robin Goodwin of Brunel University in London has been my mentor in the field of relationship research. His books, research articles and leadership in this field are unparalleled. Even before we met, whenever I would express an interest in cultural differences in close friendships at various research conferences, everyone pointed me toward Robin. I am sincerely grateful for his suggestions and expert advice.

I would like to thank members of professional organizations who allowed me to present my research at their meetings, especially The Society for International Education, Training and Research; The International Association for Relationship Researchers; and the International Association of Cross-Cultural Psychologists. These organizations include people who work in various capacities in the intercultural field, as researchers, teachers, consultants, non-governmental organization workers, aid workers of various sorts, immigration counselors, social workers, study abroad organizers, and those who work as consultants for global businesses. Talking with these professionals and gaining their feedback and ideas have helped extend and clarify my thinking. My hope is this kind of feedback will continue leading to further refinements in the framework I am proposing.

Youngmee Kim, currently at the University of Miami, was of immeasurable help with the methodological and statistical aspects of my research. She has read and commented on numerous drafts of my research articles. Eunsook Zeilfelder started out as my student, but evolved into a very insightful guide to Korean culture. Mike Whitford was my handball buddy while I was in South Korea, but also provided key insights into Korean culture.

Marty Settle, Houston Craighead, Cordelia Williams, Bert Uchino, and Maureen Ryan Griffin have read drafts of specific chapters and provided useful feedback. Marty Settle gets credit for the book's title, and Bobby Campbell for the cover image. Doug Tauchert read the entire book and provided thoughtful feedback, in addition to hassling me weekly on the handball courts. Beverly Fehr provided useful insights for the chapter on gender. Paul Foos proofread the final version.

Benjie Krauss, Leigh Ann Hallberg, Marek Ranis, Maja Godlewska, Debra Bosley, Lili Corbus, Angela Gala, Alice Momm, Cheryl Fortner-Wood, Lynn Harand, Carolyn Boyette, and Cherie Clark have encouraged me on many occasions to put these ideas about friendship into writing. Paul Bright and Marcus Keely helped with typeface and layout issues. Manoj Kasavan, Candice Langston, and Carlos Salum have been especially helpful in promoting my work here in Charlotte.

Thanks to my Brooklyn friends for offering me their apartments for weeks at a time as refuges for intensive periods of research and writing: Steve Schiff and Ana Busto, Marshall Reese and Nora Ligorano, and Nancy Bowen. And thanks to Eldred Hudson and Bob Rossier for the use of their Georgia lake house for similar purposes.

Thanks to my French friends for their many years of encouragement in this endeavor: Laurence, Frederique, Emmanuelle, Sylvia and Marceau Derai, Patrice and Christiane Schmink, Cathy Michaut, Francis and Isabelle Fordin, and Philippe Blanchard.

To date, Elisabeth Gareis has written the definitive book, based on her groundbreaking dissertation, on cultural differences in close friendships. We in this field applaud her insightful contributions to our discipline, and I am personally grateful for her thoughtful review of *Friends Beyond Borders*. Her feedback triggered a major revision in my thinking about my work.

Muriel Durand and I have shared thousands of hours, no exaggeration here, discussing all manner of cross-cultural theory, research and practice. It was her urging that motivated me to consolidate and synthesize my findings into a form that could be easily communicated. I owe her an enormous debt of gratitude and I am very proud to have her as my dear friend.

We make a living by what we get, we make a life by what we give.

–Winston Churchill

Sam Turner contributed mightily to an earlier version of the manuscript. His insightful questions and creative musings, his stream-of-consciousness style of feedback for each chapter, his suggestions regarding the organization and presentation of my ideas have all been of immeasurable value. His encouragements came at a very critical time.

Peg Robarchek has been more than an editor. Her approach as a "writing coach" has been enormously effective in helping me find "my voice" in telling my story. I am humbly grateful.

My mother-in-law Phyllis has generously allowed me to use her friendship story in Chapter Eleven, and for that I'm most grateful. Phyllis, you have been such an important and enriching part of my life over the years. You have proven what many would say is impossible, that I can have a mother-in-law as a close friend! Thank you, Phyllis.

It is with pleasure I thank my wife Susan, my very best friend, in all of the loftiest connotations and implications of that term. Susan was the last to read the entire text and her finishing touches provided just the tweaks needed to communicate my ideas more effectively. Thank you, Susan, for the grace, understanding and love you showed me through it all!

References and Chapter Notes

For a complete listing of chapter notes and full references, please go to
www.friendsbeyondbordersbook.com.

About the author

Roger Baumgarte earned his doctorate in cognitive research psychology from Bowling Green University and then taught at Winthrop University in South Carolina. For the last twenty years, he has specialized in cross-cultural psychology, focusing his research on cultural differences in close friendships.

As a popular professor, he won campus-wide awards for his work with students, and especially enjoyed serving as director of the International Center, where he advised international students coming to campus as well as U.S. students studying abroad.

Roger spent yearlong leaves of absence from Winthrop teaching at the American University in Paris and for the University of Maryland overseas program in South Korea.

He speaks fluent French, much less fluent Spanish, and a smattering of Korean, Italian, Russian, and Polish. In addition to his research on friendship, he has provided numerous workshops aimed at helping immigrants and visitors adjust to living and working in the U.S.

Made in the USA
Lexington, KY
23 November 2014